To the Rebel Girls of the world:

Believe in your dreams

Embrace your power

Unleash your magic

And always remember,

You are limitless.

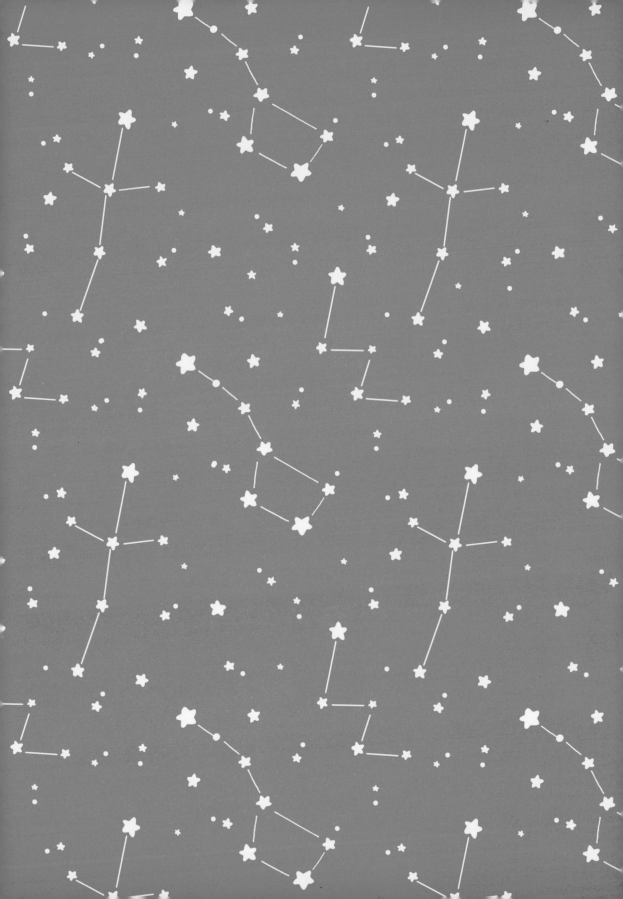

CONTENTS

~~~~~~~

FOREWORD

~~~~~~~~~

Dear Rebel,

Welcome to a book filled with Black Girl Magic! My name is CaShawn Thompson, and I am the Rebel Girl who created the popular "Black Girls Are Magic" phrase that quickly grew to become the #BlackGirlMagic movement. I'm so excited Rebel Girls asked me to participate in writing this wonderful book—and I can't wait for you to read it!

Before you dig in, I'm sure some of you may be wondering: "What is Black Girl Magic?"

I'll tell you a secret: I was just a kid myself when I realized that Black girls and women are magic. I don't mean like literal mystical creatures—more like women who do the extraordinary. As a young girl, I loved reading fairy tales filled with enchanted forests and characters with special powers, like witches, warlocks, and fairies. They were magic, so that's how I described the wonderful things happening around me.

I thought that the amazing things I saw my mom, grandma, aunts, and older cousins do were because they had special powers too! It showed up in the way my grandma baked wonderful sweet potato pies and in the way my aunt told us stories and taught me and my sister how to dance. It was also in the way my big cousins braided my hair and made us little girls feel free, loved, and strong. All those things looked and felt like magic to me.

As I've grown up and now understand the world in a more adult way, I've come to realize that what I believed to be magic as a little girl was really the hard work, intelligence, strength, and love of the Black women around me. It is magical to see them spread their light in spite of the obstacles they have faced.

Seeing those positive qualities—first in the women in my family and later in my friends, teachers, and favorite celebrities—made me feel strong and smart. I felt good about myself because I saw Black women existing in love and being examples of excellence in the world. It's important to me that young girls everywhere, of all backgrounds, girls like YOU, know about more women like this. I want YOU to be inspired and feel good too.

As you read the stories in this book, you will learn about women who are legendary as well as women who are little known. It doesn't matter how big or small their accomplishments are—each of these women is extraordinary in her own way. Some have become Olympic champions and political history makers, while others have created powerful art and remarkable inventions. You'll be amazed by them all!

Does it matter that you don't look just like they do or come from the same places that they do?

No!

Does it matter that they are older or younger than you are or speak a different language than you speak?

No way!

The only thing that matters is that YOU believe you can also achieve great things in life. These stories will expose you to phenomenal women and spark your imagination. These aren't made-up fairy tales— they are REAL-LIFE STORIES of women who are Black Girl Magic.

Just like them, you are special and important, and no matter what path you take in life, you will find the magic within yourself and share your light with the world.

I promise you, it's there.

Love always,

Ms. Shawn

CaShawn A. Thompson

INTRODUCTION

Welcome to the wondrous world of Black Girl Magic and the fourth volume of *Good Night Stories for Rebel Girls*! I'm Lilly, the editor of this book, and I'm overjoyed to invite you on this reading journey. Like each release in this series, this book is packed with 100 stories of remarkable women that will inspire you and maybe even broaden your ideas about the many things you can be and do.

There are a few things that make this volume super special. This book is all about the real-life stories of Black women, and it was created by Black people from cover to cover. More than 60 Black female or nonbinary illustrators created the incredible portraits in this book. Four Black women authors (including me!) contributed the stories. And CaShawn Thompson, the trailblazer who coined the term Black Girl Magic, helped choose the women whose stories you will find in these pages. She also wrote the foreword that begins the book.

As a storyteller with a long background in journalism, I believe it's critical to shine a bigger spotlight on the stories and legacies of Black women and girls. We've all seen Black characters in books that just don't seem real or true. Or, even worse, you've probably read lots of books that don't include Black characters at all! With this book, we want you to read about women and girls who laugh, sing, cry, and have hopes and frustrations—just like you!

The stories in this book feature women who embody four different forces. You'll read about creators like award-winning singer Aretha Franklin, champions like record-breaking tennis star Naomi Osaka, leaders like political powerhouse Shirley Chisholm, and innovators like adventurous astronaut Jeanette Epps.

As you flip through the pages, you may come across names you don't know and stories that are unfamiliar. And that's okay! Each story in this book will transport you to a different time and place, expanding your knowledge and activating your imagination. These exciting tales will take you from the Ndongo Kingdom in northern Angola in the 1600s, where Queen Nzinga went to battle to protect her country, to the steps of the White House in 2021, where Amanda Gorman became the youngest poet to speak at a presidential inauguration.

You will meet women from different continents with different complexions, hair styles, religions, backgrounds, and professions. We hope the stories will illustrate the circumstances of these women's lives, the social and personal challenges they endured, and the contributions they made. And in the back of the book, you will find a bonus section that showcases even more remarkable Black women featured in previous Rebel Girls books!

As you finish each story, take a moment to think about how each woman has inspired you. Do you want to be brave enough to lead a nation like Ethiopian empress Taytu? Or quick enough to be an Olympic fencer like Ibtihaj Muhammad? Do you want to find cool new ways to uplift your community like mushroom farmer Chido Govera?

Or blend together different types of songs to be a musical pioneer like Rosetta Tharpe? Do you want to speak up for women's rights like Funmilayo Ransome-Kuti? Or be wise like psychologist Joy Harden Bradford to help people better understand their behavior? Do you want to master the art of cooking like chef Leah Chase? Or stretch your imagination and create new worlds like author Octavia E. Butler?

These women are real-life Rebel Girls. They followed their dreams, no matter what, and they did what was right, although it may not always have been easy. Some, like journalist Ida B. Wells, witnessed horrific tragedies but still continued to write and raise awareness. Others, like investor Arlan Hamilton, struggled with homelessness before achieving success. And many, like activist Viola Desmond, had to contend with ridiculous prejudices based on the color of their skin as they tried to live rich, fulfilling lives.

These women stood up for themselves and others. And they didn't let anyone's doubts stop them from pursuing their goals.

My wish is for all of us to be like them. Let their courage and perseverance empower you and Rebel Girls everywhere to continue to shatter ceilings and soar to new heights. There's really nothing more magical than that.

With love,

Lilly

Lilly Workneh

ADRIANA BARBOSA

ENTREPRENEUR

When Adriana was a kid, her great-grandmother gave her a piece of advice: "Sell today. Eat tomorrow." At the marketplace in São Paulo, Brazil, Adriana saw exactly what she meant. She watched women sitting at small, colorful stands selling food. If they didn't sell, their families' bellies would be empty.

Adriana started her first job at 15 to help out her family. But at 25, she found herself unemployed and out of money. So she set up a thrift store on the side of the road. Sitting there in the hot sun, she made friends with a fellow vendor who sold pastries. Together, they dreamed up a fantastic idea and decided to bring it to life. They would launch a market to promote Black businesses.

The first Feira Preta, or "Black Market," opened in 2002 with 40 vendors. They sold a little bit of everything: hair oils, headwraps, natural beauty products, patterned fabrics, crafts, toys, shoes, and more. Five thousand visitors came in a single weekend!

More people and more vendors crammed into the market each year until Adriana had to find a bigger venue. Feira Preta grew into a 20-day celebration of Black art, culture, and science, with speeches and even political debates. Twenty years later, the fair is still going strong.

Adriana started a training program for Black business owners, hosted events to bring entrepreneurs together, and set up a platform so Feira Preta vendors could sell online. With creativity and vision, she supports Black business owners and helps their companies thrive.

BORN AUGUST 28, 1977
BRAZIL

ILLUSTRATION BY
MARINA VENANCIO

"WE HAVE A VERY STRONG
ENTREPRENEURIAL VEIN.
IT IS IN OUR DNA."
—ADRIANA BARBOSA

ALEXA CANADY

PEDIATRIC NEUROSURGEON

Once upon a time, there was a girl who was *really* smart. But nobody knew it, because her test scores were just okay.

Alexa's family did a little digging to find out why she didn't test well at school. They found out that Alexa's elementary school teacher had been switching her grades with a white student's. The wicked teacher got fired, and Alexa skipped third grade and went straight to fourth.

In college, Alexa started out in the math department, but something was missing. Next, she got a degree in zoology, the study of animals. But that wasn't a perfect fit either. Finally, she found medicine, and it was just right! Alexa realized she wanted to heal people.

After years and years of training, she became the first Black woman to be a pediatric neurosurgeon—a doctor who treats children's brains.

Alexa loved her job. Sometimes she'd work as many as 100 hours in a week, playing games with patients, diagnosing them, and battling their illnesses. She healed thousands of children. Some kids were in her care for so long that she became part of their family. Her patients trusted her and told her about their symptoms. Sometimes even the littlest bits of information could make a big difference in saving a kid's life.

Once, a little boy came to her showing signs of a stroke. Alexa didn't believe it. He was so young! How could he have a disease that usually only affected adults? Something didn't feel right to Alexa.

After many tests, she found a tiny tumor. She removed it and saved the boy's life. "Always trust your gut," Alexa says.

BORN NOVEMBER 7, 1950
UNITED STATES OF AMERICA

ILLUSTRATION BY
TAYLOR MCMANUS

"THE MOST DIFFICULT
STEP TO ACCOMPLISHING
SOMETHING IS BELIEVING
IT IS POSSIBLE."
—ALEXA CANADY

ALICIA GARZA, OPAL TOMETI, AND PATRISSE CULLORS

ACTIVISTS

Like many people across the nation, Alicia paid attention to a court case involving the death of a young Black boy named Trayvon Martin. After three weeks, the verdict came in. And the man responsible for Trayvon's death was set free. Alicia was outraged. On July 13, 2013, she posted on Facebook: "Black people. I love you. I love us. Our lives matter."

Her friend Patrisse replied and added the hashtag #BlackLivesMatter. A mighty movement was born.

People nationwide used the hashtag on social media. They talked about the unequal treatment of Black people. Soon the conversation turned into action. Patrisse co-led a bus ride for more than 600 people from cities across the country to Ferguson, Missouri, where another young Black man had been killed.

Alicia and Patrisse's Nigerian American friend, Opal, knew what they were doing was important. She thought the movement needed a platform, a place where people could connect and collaborate. So these three innovative organizers formed a global network with more than 40 chapters. The groups work locally to challenge injustices against Black communities, support Black culture and art, and celebrate Black joy. #BlackLivesMatter has brought countless people together to fight for equality—to march, protest, sign petitions, and vote for change.

ALICIA GARZA, BORN JANUARY 4, 1981
OPAL TOMETI, BORN AUGUST 15, 1984
PATRISSE CULLORS, BORN JUNE 20, 1983

UNITED STATES OF AMERICA

"WE ARE A GENERATION CALLED TO ACTION."
—PATRISSE CULLORS

ILLUSTRATION BY
NAKI NARH

AMANDA GORMAN

POET

Once there was a girl who had no idea that, one day, she would wow the world with her words.

As a child, Amanda realized she couldn't hear like other kids did. She wasn't learning to read at the same pace as her classmates. And she had trouble saying certain sounds. But she didn't let those challenges stop her from expressing herself.

In the third grade, her teacher introduced her to poetry. Amanda loved how beautifully the words could paint scenes, create characters, and bring messages to life. Writing poetry came naturally to Amanda. And reading her poems aloud helped her practice her speaking skills.

In her powerful poems, Amanda advocated for change in the world. In high school, she began to win awards for her work. She even became the first-ever National Youth Poet Laureate—an enormous honor!

At 22 years old, Amanda received the invitation of a lifetime. She was asked to write a poem for the 2021 US presidential inauguration.

On a cold January day, she stood before the crowd and cameras. The wind whipped around her as her excitement swirled inside her head. After a pause, Amanda opened her mouth. She held her arms outstretched and, with a strong, clear voice, she delivered a poem that called for hope, **diversity**, and unity in the country. The world watched in awe.

New to fame, Amanda said, "I am learning that I am not lightning that strikes once. I am the hurricane that comes every single year, and you can expect to see me again soon."

BORN MARCH 7, 1998
UNITED STATES OF AMERICA

"THE ONLY THING THAT CAN IMPEDE ME IS MYSELF."
—AMANDA GORMAN

ILLUSTRATION BY KETURAH ARIEL

ANDREA JENKINS

POET AND POLITICIAN

Once there was a child who learned to speak up, even when it was scary. Doctors said the child was a boy, but the child felt uncomfortable wearing boy clothes and being called a boy name. The child knew she was a girl.

So in her early thirties, she transitioned. She changed her name to Andrea and put on the clothes she'd always wanted to wear.

Some people were mean to her. But Andrea held her head up high and kept doing what she always did: she used her creative mind to craft beautiful poetry and fight for the equal treatment of all people.

Andrea had a big heart and a passion for justice. While working for the Minneapolis city government, she recorded hundreds of stories from **transgender** and gender nonconforming people across the Midwest. She worked on a book series that showcased LGBTQIA+ voices. She also published a few poetry books of her own, including *The T Is Not Silent*.

In 2016, a city council member in her district retired, leaving a seat open. Andrea knew it was her moment. She ran for city council . . . and won! She made history by becoming the first Black trans woman to be elected to the city council of a major city.

"Having transgender people elected in public office means we'll be able to make policies and direct conversations," Andrea said. "[We] can ensure equity and fairness and justice for transgender people."

And she's doing just that, one law at a time.

BORN MAY 10, 1961
UNITED STATES OF AMERICA

ILLUSTRATION BY
KELSEE THOMAS

"I KNOW FIRSTHAND
THE FEELING OF BEING
MARGINALIZED, LEFT OUT,
THROWN UNDER THE BUS.
THOSE DAYS ARE OVER.
WE DON'T JUST WANT
A SEAT AT THE TABLE—
WE WANT TO SET
THE TABLE."
—ANDREA JENKINS

ANGELA DAVIS

ACTIVIST

Once upon a time in Birmingham, Alabama, there lived a girl named Angela who had a fire in her. She was frustrated by the **racism** she saw every day and knew she had to fight for freedom and justice.

She armed herself with knowledge that struck her like lightning, she said, fueling her passion for **liberation**. She got a job as a professor at a university and joined political groups like the Black Panthers and the Communist party. Some people thought these groups were dangerous. When Angela's bosses found out she was a member, they fired her.

Angela threw herself into activism. She wanted to bring an end to racism and other injustices Black people faced. She ran a campaign to free political prisoners—people who were imprisoned for their beliefs. She vowed not to stop until all Black people were free.

Soon Angela herself became a political prisoner. She was accused of being involved in a crime, even though she was nowhere nearby when it took place. The police threw her in jail anyway.

Protestors chanted outside the barbed wire fence surrounding the prison. "Free Angela and all political prisoners!" they shouted. After nearly 20 long months, the court decided Angela was innocent.

To pass the time while she was stuck behind bars, she wrote her first book. Angela continues to write, speak, and teach about liberation. "You have to act as if it were possible to radically transform the world," she says. "And you have to do it all the time."

BORN JANUARY 26, 1944
UNITED STATES OF AMERICA

ILLUSTRATION BY
SARAH MADDEN

"I AM NO LONGER
ACCEPTING THE THINGS
I CANNOT CHANGE. I AM
CHANGING THE THINGS
I CANNOT ACCEPT."
—ANGELA DAVIS

ANGELA JAMES

HOCKEY PLAYER

Once upon a time, there was a girl who was sweet and nice but vicious on the ice! Her name was Angela.

She grew up in a tough neighborhood in Toronto and stayed active by playing street hockey with her sisters. She loved it! She ran around with a hockey stick and slapped the black puck into the net, scoring goal after goal.

There weren't any girls' or women's ice hockey leagues near her. So her mother signed her up for the boys' league.

Angela proved to everyone that she was just as good as the boys—and better than most. She was so good, in fact, that she was holding her own on the ice with boys who were three years older than her.

Sadly, after just one year, Angela was kicked off the team. The reason was clear to Angela: the league didn't like that the best player on a boys' team was a girl!

Later, Angela joined a girls' league. She had to take a long bus ride to attend her games, but she didn't mind. She'd do anything to play! Soon the Central Ontario Women's Hockey League invited 16-year-old Angela to join a team. With her helmet and skates, she was ready to go!

Angela was a powerhouse on the ice—an unstoppable force when she headed for the goal. She played for 20 years, racking up wins and gold medals. Her record-breaking skills landed her in the Hockey Hall of Fame, where she made history as the first Black woman and the first openly gay player to be inducted.

BORN DECEMBER 22, 1964

CANADA

"YOU CAN DO WHAT YOU WANT TO ACCOMPLISH BY BEING YOU. DON'T FEEL THAT YOU HAVE TO BE SOMEBODY ELSE."
—ANGELA JAMES

ILLUSTRATION BY
KATELUN C. BREWSTER

ANGELLA DOROTHEA FERGUSON

MEDICAL RESEARCHER

In high school, Angella discovered the magic of chemistry. Even though her family was poor, she attended a prestigious university. Her parents saved up enough money for her first year. By working summers and earning scholarships, she paid for the rest.

During this time, many Black women found work as housekeepers and secretaries. But Angella wanted to be a scientist and a doctor. Her favorite class was pediatrics. So she decided to work in children's health and opened her own clinic. When Black parents asked questions like "When should my baby start walking?" Angella realized she didn't have the answers. Up until then, research on child development had focused on white children.

With a former professor, Angella began detailed studies of Black infants and their development. Soon she discovered a problem: many of the children suffered from a disease called sickle cell anemia. Healthy red blood cells are shaped like donuts. They carry oxygen throughout the body. But diseased cells fold into a C shape that looks like a farm tool called a sickle. These cells can block blood flow. When this happens, children can experience severe pain and even die.

Angella studied hundreds of cases. Finally, she identified the signs of sickle cell disease. She urged Black parents to get their children tested for it at birth. She also developed effective treatments, such as drinking soda water to prevent pain.

Angella used her magic to improve the health of Black families.

BORN FEBRUARY 15, 1925
UNITED STATES OF AMERICA

ILLUSTRATION BY
LYDIA MBA

"THOSE WHO WANT A
CAREER SHOULD HAVE THE
OPPORTUNITY FOR ONE."
—ANGELLA DOROTHEA FERGUSON

ANNA OLGA ALBERTINA BROWN

AERIALIST

Once upon a time in Prussia, now known as Poland, there was a young **biracial** performer named Anna. Tiny and incredibly strong, Anna joined the circus when she was nine years old. She quickly mastered the tightrope, trapeze, and other daring acts.

Under the stage name Miss La La, Anna dazzled audiences across Europe as an aerealist. In her unforgettable "iron jaw" act, she used a thick leather strap with a mouthpiece on one end and a hook on the other. She hooked the leather strap to the trapeze and bit down on the mouthpiece. Dangling by her teeth high in the air, she spun and spun!

Next Anna hung from the trapeze by her knees. With the leather strap between her teeth, she supported another trapeze. On it, a child, a woman, a man, and finally a duo took turns striking poses.

She had more moves to shock the crowd. Hanging upside down, dangling by just one knee, she held three men: one in each arm—and one supported by her teeth! Then came the grand finale. Anna lifted a brass cannon by a strap held in her mouth, then—*BOOM!*—the cannon fired. Her body flew back from the blast. She astounded the audience as she still held up the smoking cannon.

The famous French artist Edgar Degas was so captivated by Anna's high-flying act that he painted her. The grace and strength of Europe's first Black female circus star was forever captured on canvas.

APRIL 21, 1858–AFTER 1919

POLAND

ILLUSTRATION BY
TONI D. CHAMBERS

ANNE-MARIE IMAFIDON

MATHEMATICIAN

One day in East London, a girl named Anne-Marie typed out the story "Little Red Riding Hood" on the computer. She changed the color of the famous red cloak and saved the story as "Little Purple Riding Hood." The next day, her creation was still there! That's when she fell in love with technology.

Growing up, Anne-Marie didn't write or draw much. Instead, her creativity shone when she built websites on her father's computer.

She took apart electronics to figure out how they worked. A clever child, Anne-Marie knew most of the answers in class and quickly grew bored. The school moved her ahead. At 11, she became the youngest girl to pass A-level computing—an exam British students usually take at 16.

In college, Anne-Marie was one of only three girls studying mathematics and computer science. Once, she attended a conference celebrating women in computing. She'd never seen so many female technologists!

Worried about the small number of women entering the fields of science, technology, engineering, and mathematics (STEM), Anne-Marie cofounded a group called Stemettes.

At Stemettes events, girls experiment and have fun, learning how to code and hack. Stemettes hosts workshops where teams create their own apps to solve problems, like helping **refugees** communicate in English or providing students with reminders to get to class on time.

Many girls say they don't pursue STEM studies because they don't see women doing "sciency things." Anne-Marie hopes to change that.

BORN JUNE 24, 1989
UNITED KINGDOM

$Q = cm$

$V = \dfrac{m}{M} = \dfrac{N}{N_A}$

$\phi = BS\cos(B_n)$

ILLUSTRATION BY
MAYA EALEY

$V - V_0 = \beta V_0(t - t_0)$

$pV = R1$

$\dfrac{v^2}{c^2}$

"OUR RETELLING OF
SCIENTIFIC *HISTORY* IS
MISSING THE *HER*STORY."
—ANNE-MARIE IMAFIDON

ARETHA FRANKLIN

SINGER

Once upon a time, there was a girl who turned her feelings into breathtaking, soulful music.

Aretha hated being told what to do. In fact, when her first piano teacher came to her house, she hid instead of taking a lesson. She sang at her father's church and put on shows at home with the family grand piano. "Oh, that child sure can sing!" everyone said.

No one knew where Aretha's incredible sound came from, but some say it was from all the things she witnessed in her life—that she funneled her pain and heartache into raw, passionate music like a magic spell.

In one of her songs, she demanded what she knew she deserved: "a little respect." Her song "Respect" resonated with women who had been hurt by men. It resonated with Black people who had been humiliated by racists. It became a rallying cry of the **civil rights movement**.

Aretha honed her talent and stage presence. She mastered singing gospel, jazz, blues, and R&B. Once, with less than a day's notice, she stepped in for famous opera singer Luciano Pavarotti during the 1998 Grammy Awards. He was too sick to perform. So Aretha sang the famous aria "Nessun dorma" in a room packed with celebrated musicians. When she was done, they leaped to their feet and gave her an unforgettable standing ovation. The "Queen of Soul" got the respect she deserved!

By the end of her career, Aretha had 43 Top 40 singles, 18 Grammy Awards, and 20 number one R&B hits. She was the first woman inducted into the Rock & Roll Hall of Fame.

MARCH 25, 1942–AUGUST 16, 2018
UNITED STATES OF AMERICA

ILLUSTRATION BY
JOHNALYNN HOLLAND

"SOUL TO ME IS
A FEELING, A LOT
OF DEPTH, AND BEING
ABLE TO BRING TO THE
SURFACE THAT WHICH IS
HAPPENING INSIDE."
—ARETHA FRANKLIN

ARIAM TEKLE

PODCAST HOST AND DOCUMENTARY FILMMAKER

Ariam had a childhood filled with questions about who she really was. She grew up in Milan, a city in northern Italy. But her parents were from an East African country called Eritrea. In the 1970s, they moved to Italy, where Ariam was born.

Growing up, she did not see people like her in Italian stories or on the news. Most people she met assumed she was not Italian at all. She wondered if other Eritrean Italians had similar experiences. So she decided to ask them.

While in university, Ariam produced a documentary film that told the stories of **second-generation** Eritreans and how they had trouble being accepted. "We are talking about a generation that has remained in the shadows," she said, "an invisible generation." Some people were shy at first. But they opened up and began to tell Ariam their stories.

A few years later, Ariam and a friend started a podcast called *#BlackCoffee*. It was a space for them to discuss their identity and the hardships Black Italians face.

In 2020, protests against police brutality erupted all over the United States. The protests sparked similar demonstrations in other countries, including Italy. Suddenly, Ariam noticed that a lot more people were tuning in to *#BlackCoffee*. Her show had become an important outlet for Italians looking to learn and do more in the fight against **racism**.

No longer a little girl grappling with questions all alone, Ariam has united people so they may tackle challenges together.

BORN OCTOBER 14, 1988

ITALY

ILLUSTRATION BY
AURÉLIA DURAND

"WE HAVE ALWAYS HAD [OUR OWN]
LANGUAGE TO TALK ABOUT SYSTEMIC
RACISM. THE DIFFERENCE IS THAT THE
WORLD IS FINALLY LISTENING."
—ARIAM TEKLE

ARLAN HAMILTON

INVESTOR

Arlan was a curious and ambitious girl. As a child, she earned money by selling candy to her classmates. That was her first business venture! When she was 20, she created her own magazine.

Arlan dreamed of working in the music industry, so she decided to skip college and travel with a band. In her adventures as a tour manager, she met and learned from people with all types of backgrounds. The world had become her classroom!

After years of touring, Arlan was ready to start a new business. She had heard of people who invest money in companies just starting out. These investors are called venture capitalists. They provide funds, and in return, they own a percentage of the companies they invest in. Arlan wanted to do that too. But she really wanted to invest in companies led by people like her—people who were often overlooked.

To become a venture capitalist, Arlan needed money and lots of it. She did a ton of research and identified people who might fund her plan to support diverse businesses. She began reaching out to investors. Success did not come overnight. She stayed on friends' couches and sometimes even slept on the airport floor.

After three years, Arlan got her first yes! Someone invested $25,000, and her company, Backstage Capital, was born. Arlan is the only gay Black woman to build a venture capital firm from the ground up. She has since invested more than $7 million in more than 130 companies, giving them a much-needed push.

BORN OCTOBER 30, 1980
UNITED STATES OF AMERICA

ILLUSTRATION BY
OLIVIA FIELDS

"BE YOURSELF SO
THAT THE PEOPLE
LOOKING FOR YOU
CAN FIND YOU."
—ARLAN HAMILTON

AUDRE LORDE

POET

Once there was a girl who didn't speak until she was four years old. Audre listened carefully, though, and what finally came out of her mouth was beautiful.

Audre learned early that words have power. In high school, she memorized famous lines from great poets. But eventually, borrowed words were not enough. The budding poet and her school friends, all of them daughters of **immigrants**, formed a group called "The Branded." Audre's parents were from Barbados and Grenada.

She worked many jobs while she studied to become a librarian, and in 1968, she published her first collection of poems called *The First Cities*. Audre beamed with joy as she read from the pages of her crisp new book full of enchanting words. Her words.

She put out a new poetry collection every two years until 1978, when her masterpiece, *The Black Unicorn*, hit bookstores. That same year, she was diagnosed with breast cancer and began the fight of her life. She wrote about her illness and pain. She hoped that others struggling with cancer wouldn't feel so alone.

Audre did not just write pretty words. Her words called for social change, acceptance, and celebration of difference. Together with a group of writer friends, she started a publishing company called Kitchen Table: Women of Color Press to raise up women's voices.

She described herself as "Black, feminist, lesbian, mother, warrior, poet," and she will always be remembered for her fearless words.

FEBRUARY 18, 1934–NOVEMBER 17, 1992
UNITED STATES OF AMERICA

"WHEN WE SPEAK, WE ARE AFRAID OUR WORDS WILL NOT BE HEARD OR WELCOMED. BUT WHEN WE ARE SILENT, WE ARE STILL AFRAID. SO IT IS BETTER TO SPEAK."
—AUDRE LORDE

ILLUSTRATION BY KELSEE THOMAS

AUGUSTA SAVAGE

SCULPTOR

Once, in Florida, there was a girl named Augusta who had 13 siblings but not a single toy. She loved digging her hands into the red clay in her backyard. Instead of making mud pies, she'd mold the clay into ducks and other animals.

At 29 years old, with little money but lots of encouragement, Augusta moved to Harlem, a Black neighborhood in New York City. There, she studied at a prestigious art school tuition-free.

Many artists at that time portrayed Black people with exaggerated features. Augusta and other **Harlem Renaissance** artists rejected those offensive depictions. Instead, she created sculptures that showed Black people in a realistic way.

Augusta earned a scholarship to an art school in Paris. But when the selection committee found out she was Black, they withdrew the offer. Augusta spoke out about it. She said she was standing up not only for herself but for future students of color. Six years later, Augusta made it to Paris with another grant! She exhibited her art and won awards.

When she returned to the US, she transformed her studio into a free school where she mentored future master artists. For the 1939 World's Fair, she made a remarkable 16-foot sculpture nicknamed *The Harp*. In it, 12 singing Black children stand on the hand of God, as if they are the strings of a harp. Like many of her works, *The Harp* didn't survive, because she didn't have the money to cast it in bronze. The daring beauty of her existing sculptures, however, remains an inspiration to all.

FEBRUARY 29, 1892–MARCH 26, 1962
UNITED STATES OF AMERICA

"HOW AM I TO COMPETE WITH OTHER AMERICAN ARTISTS IF I'M NOT TO BE GIVEN THE SAME OPPORTUNITY?"
—AUGUSTA SAVAGE

ILLUSTRATION BY CHERISE HARRIS

AVA DUVERNAY

FILMMAKER

Once upon a time, there was a girl named Ava who loved to make up stories. She and her sisters would spend entire days using their dolls to act out the wild tales they dreamed up.

Ava thought she would use her storytelling skills to become an investigative reporter. But after college, she landed a job at a movie studio, where she learned what it took to weave enchanting tales on film. Ava was hooked! She knew how meaningful movies could be.

Ava noticed that a lot of films by people of color weren't getting the attention they deserved. So she launched her own publicity firm. She worked with Black, **Latinx**, Native American, and women filmmakers to make sure *lots* of people saw their films.

When Ava was 32 years old, she picked up a camera for the first time. She didn't have any experience, but that didn't keep her from directing her own stories in her own way. She was a fast learner—and within a few years, Ava released her first feature film!

Soon everyone knew her name. She produced and directed dozens of films and TV shows, and many of them were centered around the experiences and history of Black people in America. Ava won awards and became the first Black woman to direct a film with a budget of $100 million.

She has paved the way for more women like her. As the head of her own film company, she champions films by women and people of color. With an eye to the future, she has said, "I will be there for whoever's next."

BORN AUGUST 24, 1972
UNITED STATES OF AMERICA

ILLUSTRATION BY
ADESEWA ADEKOYA

"DON'T WAIT FOR PERMISSION
TO DO SOMETHING CREATIVE."
—AVA DUVERNAY

AYA CISSOKO

BOXER

Once there was a girl named Aya who didn't give up when life knocked her down. Her parents emigrated from Mali, in West Africa, to France. They all lived together in a one-room apartment. They were poor, but with her siblings, toys, and school, Aya was happy.

When she was eight, Aya suffered a terrible tragedy. She lost her father and sister. Less than a year later, her brother fell ill and also passed away. Aya found strength by playing sports.

She practiced archery, judo, and swimming, but she loved boxing most of all. In the ring, she released the pain she wasn't able to express with words. "It saved me," she said. "Boxing allowed me to stand up."

Though her mother wasn't happy about her interest in a "boys' sport," Aya started intense training: running, doing push-ups, and practicing punches. At 12, she won her first French championship.

Later, she became a French, a European, and then a three-time world champion—but she still earned less than a man! She worked nine hours a day as an accountant while training six days a week.

In 2008, tragedy struck again. Aya was seriously hurt during a boxing match and ended up paralyzed on one side of her body. But she was resilient. She learned to walk and use her arm again. She wrote about her life in a book titled *Danbé*, which means "dignity," and encouraged readers to keep going even during rough times.

In the book, Aya wrote a lot about her mother. She realized that her mother's courage and self-respect had always been her inspiration.

BORN NOVEMBER 23, 1978
FRANCE

"THERE IS NOTHING MORE
IMPORTANT THAN DANBÉ."
—AYA CISSOKO

ILLUSTRATION BY
SARAH LOULENDO

BARBARA HILLARY

NURSE AND ADVENTURER

Barbara was always a curious kid. Lucky for her, that curiosity never went away. After 55 years as a full-time nurse and part-time taxi driver, she was ready for a new adventure.

She wanted to visit all the places she'd never had the time or money to see before. Did she start out with a quiet trip to a sunny beach? Not Barbara! She booked herself a trip to Canada in the middle of winter.

There, she photographed humongous polar bears and learned how to dogsled across frozen fields. Loving the snowy landscape, she decided to become the first Black woman to reach the North Pole.

To prepare, Barbara collected fleece clothes, took lots of vitamins, ran miles on the treadmill, and pumped iron at the gym. She took skiing lessons and raised money for supplies. Then she hired guides to help her across the ever-shifting ice floes.

Barbara took two bumpy helicopter rides to get close to the North Pole. The gear she carried was heavy, and the journey was longer and colder than any she'd made before. And because of a cancer surgery she'd had a few years before, her lungs weren't the best. But she didn't let that stop her. Seventy-five-year-old Barbara skied the rest of the way.

When she reached the North Pole, she jumped up and down and screamed into the frosty air. She'd made it to the top of the world!

And she wasn't done yet. Right before her 80th birthday, Barbara trekked to the South Pole. Her adventurous spirit took her all over the world, and she loved every minute of it!

 JUNE 12, 1931–NOVEMBER 23, 2019
UNITED STATES OF AMERICA

"AT EVERY PHASE IN YOUR LIFE, LOOK AT YOUR OPTIONS. PLEASE, DO NOT SELECT BORING ONES."
—BARBARA HILLARY

ILLUSTRATION BY AMARI MITNAUL

BESSIE COLEMAN

PILOT

Bessie was born into a big family. Her mother, an African American maid, and her father, a Black Native American **sharecropper**, raised 13 children. Bessie spent most of her childhood helping her mother pick cotton and wash laundry to make money.

Bessie couldn't afford college, so she moved to Chicago to live with her brothers. There, she studied to become a beautician and worked at a local barbershop.

Bessie's brothers were army veterans, and they would often share stories about fighting in France during World War I. They poked fun at her because French women could learn how to fly airplanes and Bessie could not. Fed up with their teasing, she applied to flight school. Sadly, her applications were denied because she was Black and a woman.

Bessie came up with a plan. She signed up for night classes to learn French and sent messages across the ocean. Soon she was on her way to France to earn her international pilot's license!

Not only did Bessie learn to fly planes, but she also learned how to do tricks. She could fly planes upside down, make cool loops, and draw figure eights in the air. She gave dazzling performances. People came from all over to watch her. Bessie performed only in places that did not segregate Black and white spectators.

Her dream was to open a flight school for Black students. But tragically, Bessie died young. Still, her time in the pilot's seat showed what a bold Black woman could do.

JANUARY 26, 1892–APRIL 30, 1926
UNITED STATES OF AMERICA

BESSIE STRINGFIELD

MOTORCYCLIST

Once upon a time, a young woman named Bessie received the most extraordinary gift: a motorcycle.

She was 16 years old. It wasn't very "ladylike," according to the big gossips around town. She ignored them and revved her engine with a mighty roar. Exhaust smoke trailed behind her like an old friend.

At 19, Bessie was tired of riding around the same old streets. She pulled out a map, closed her eyes, and flipped a penny. Wherever it landed, Bessie went. Her hair spilled out from beneath her helmet, catching the wind and light, as she crisscrossed her way around the country, visiting 48 states in total.

But the country was still segregated. On the road, Bessie couldn't sleep in motels or eat at any diner she passed. Instead, she relied on the kindness of Black families in the towns she visited or slept on her bike under the stars. She shrugged when people asked her about the dangers of being a Black woman on the road.

"I had my ups and downs," she said.

In her lifetime, Bessie owned 27 motorcycles, and each one had a story. With one, she performed a stunt known as the wall of death, where she raced around the inside of a giant metal globe, even riding upside down! And she rode more than a few in the Orange Blossom Parade in Miami, Florida, where she lived for many years.

Well into her seventies, Bessie rode her blue motorcycle to church. The Motorcycle Queen of Miami charted her own course.

CIRCA 1911–FEBRUARY 16, 1993
UNITED STATES OF AMERICA

"I SPENT MOST OF MY LIFE ALONE, LOOKIN' FOR A FAMILY. I FOUND MY FAMILY IN MOTORCYCLING."
—BESSIE STRINGFIELD

ILLUSTRATION BY KIM HOLT

BEVERLY LORAINE GREENE

ARCHITECT

Beverly was an only child. She often had to keep herself busy while her father went to work at a law firm and her mother managed the house. Beverly's favorite thing to do was draw. With lines and curves and color, she could make pictures come to life.

After high school, she studied architecture. But university life was not easy for Beverly. She stood out in her classes. When she graduated, she was the first Black woman at her university to get a degree in architectural engineering. And when she registered as an architect with the state of Illinois in 1942, she became the first licensed Black woman architect in the United States. She could now draw and design all the buildings she wanted! Or so she thought.

Despite all her achievements, Beverly could not find a job in her hometown. No one in Chicago would hire a Black female architect.

So she packed her bags and moved to New York City. She applied for a job with a company building a housing project. The company did not want Black people living in their houses, and Beverly thought they'd never hire a Black architect. But she applied for the job anyway. To her great surprise, she got the job. Her career had begun!

Beverly worked on the designs for an arts complex, a university theater, a United Nations headquarters in Paris, and even the funeral home where her memorial service was held.

The little girl who loved to draw grew up to design beautiful buildings and break barriers for Black women.

OCTOBER 4, 1915–AUGUST 22, 1957
UNITED STATES OF AMERICA

ILLUSTRATION BY
ASHLEIGH CORRIN

BREE NEWSOME BASS

ACTIVIST

Bree was a born leader. In high school, she served as class president for three years. During her senior year, she was elected student body president.

She always stood up for what she believed in. Once, she said that just being herself was "an act of defiance."

When she was 28 years old, Bree protested against her local senator for supporting a bill that made it difficult for people to cast their votes in elections. That's when Bree began to see herself as an activist.

Then, in July 2015, a terrible shooting shook the country. It was a horrific act of racist violence. Heartbroken, Bree knew she needed to take a stand. Within days, she'd trained with other activists and was ready to go. She marched to the South Carolina statehouse and looked up at the Confederate flag waving in the air. She had always been upset to see the Confederate flag on state property because she—along with many others—see it as a symbol of **racism** and hatred toward Black people.

Bree knew her defiant act would result in her arrest. But it was worth it. Wearing a harness, she climbed up the 30-foot pole. She gripped the flag tightly in her hands and tore it down. Cheers rang out as she returned safely to the ground.

A short time later, the Confederate flag was officially removed from the South Carolina statehouse, as well as from several other places across the nation. By taking down a symbol of the past, Bree became a symbol for the future.

BORN MAY 13, 1985
UNITED STATES OF AMERICA

ILLUSTRATION BY
AURÉLIA DURAND

"EVERYONE IN THE
COMMUNITY HAS
A ROLE TO PLAY."
—BREE NEWSOME BASS

BRIGID KOSGEI

MARATHON RUNNER

As a little girl, Brigid walked six miles to school every day. Sometimes she would jog to avoid being late. Along the way, she would see athletes running gracefully in single file, training for races and marathons. She wanted to be just like them.

Brigid always took part in running events at school. Unfortunately, in her third year of high school, Brigid's mother could no longer afford to pay her school fees. She had to drop out of school at 17 years old. Suddenly, Brigid found she had a lot of time to dedicate to running.

The budding athlete started training seriously with her boyfriend, who soon became her husband. After the pair got married, Brigid gave birth to twins and took a break from her athletic career.

A year later, she returned to her training, more motivated than ever.

Brigid's specialty was running long distances, like marathons, which are 26.2 miles long! To succeed, Brigid had to be physically fit and mentally focused. She would remind herself, "Sometimes you have to be more patient than others, and sometimes you may not feel like running, but in the end, it will pay off."

And it sure did.

In Portugal in 2015, Brigid ran her very first marathon. And she won first place! In 2019, at 25 years old, Brigid became the youngest woman ever to win the London Marathon. That same year, she won the Chicago Marathon, breaking the world record by 81 seconds!

Brigid is the fastest female marathon runner in the world.

BORN FEBRUARY 20, 1994
KENYA

ILLUSTRATION BY
DATA ORUWARI

"CONSISTENCY IS KEY."
—BRIGID KOSGEI

CAROLINA CONTRERAS

NATURAL HAIR STYLIST AND ENTREPRENEUR

Once upon a time, there lived a girl who battled her own hair. For as long as she could remember, Carolina had straightened her hair. Her mother believed it gave Carolina a better chance at succeeding in life. So she would relax and straighten her daughter's hair to make Carolina look "presentable."

As she got older, Carolina started to question why she felt she had to spend so much time and effort changing her hair. *Why can't my hair remain natural and still be pretty?* she thought.

Carolina was born in the Dominican Republic and grew up in the United States. At 21, Carolina took her first trip back to her birth country. It was so hot and humid there that she found it challenging to maintain her straight hair. All she wanted to do was to feel comfortable. She was tired of trying to be "acceptable." So she cut all her hair off.

Carolina's trip to the Dominican Republic was meant to last only two months, but she ended up settling there for more than nine years. Learning to care for her natural hair inspired her to start writing a blog. The blog became so popular that it started a movement to empower women to love themselves as they are.

Carolina then opened the first all-natural hair salon in the Dominican Republic. The salon not only takes expert care of natural curls but also provides a safe space for Black and **Latinx** women to feel beautiful, confident, and comfortable with their natural hair.

BORN DECEMBER 3, 1986

DOMINICAN REPUBLIC AND UNITED STATES OF AMERICA

ILLUSTRATION BY
JEANETTA GONZALES

"ONCE GIRLS LEAVE THE SALON,
YOU CAN SEE THEM SKIPPING.
THEY'RE STANDING A LITTLE
TALLER, THEY'RE SWAYING THEIR
HAIR SIDE TO SIDE."
—CAROLINA CONTRERAS

CHIDO GOVERA

MUSHROOM FARMER

Chido was born in a poverty-stricken part of Zimbabwe. She had a difficult childhood. She became an orphan at the age of seven and dropped out of school at the age of nine to take care of her younger brother and her blind grandmother. As a way to make money, she looked after a field of crops. She tried to grow different vegetables, like maize—but they all failed.

When she was 11, she attended a program that changed her life and her community forever. There, she learned about oyster mushrooms. Mushrooms are not just a food, she discovered. They also help other crops grow and provide income to people who tend to them.

Chido put her new knowledge to work. And less than a week after she returned home from the program, she had her first harvest! She cooked up her mushrooms and served them with small pieces of chicken. She sold her dishes, and customers loved them! Soon Chido earned enough money to feed her family and send her brother—along with other orphans—to school.

In time, Chido earned enough to return to school herself. She learned to speak English and studied the science of mushrooms more deeply, marveling at how they can be used to remove toxins from soil and water. She has since traveled around the world to study medicinal mushrooms too.

Learning about mushrooms transformed Chido's life. Now she transforms the lives of others through education and job opportunities.

BORN 1986
ZIMBABWE

"I'VE BEEN ABLE TO RECLAIM MYSELF. THIS IS SOMETHING THAT'S REQUIRED FOR EVERY INDIVIDUAL. WE ARE NOT WHAT HAPPENED TO US."
—CHIDO GOVERA

ILLUSTRATION BY NAOMI ANDERSON-SUBRYAN

CLARA HALE

HUMANITARIAN

Some people called Clara a saint, but she was just a woman who never turned away a person in need.

Clara became an orphan in her teens and a widow after just three years of marriage. She had three children, started a day care, and opened her home in New York City to **foster** children. By age 64, Clara had fostered 40 kids! After she retired, she thought she'd slow down, but one day, a mother arrived at her door with a sick baby.

Clara worried about caring for a child with such serious needs. But the mother gave her no choice. She abandoned the wailing child. A few days later, the mother dropped off the rest of her children as well.

Clara did what she did best: she cared for them all.

Word got out that she would take on even the most difficult cases. Some children arrived so ill that Clara stayed up all night to soothe them. She sang to them, played with them, and read to them. Then she helped the parents learn to care for them too.

The community took care of "Mother Hale." They donated clothes, food, and money to her and the children. She always had everything she needed. Eventually, the need for her program grew so large she applied for money from the government. With it, she bought a five-story brownstone that neighbors called Hale House.

After Clara passed away, her daughter, Dr. Lorraine Hale, carried on her **legacy**. She said, "As long as there are babies in need of love and care, Hale House must be here to meet their needs."

APRIL 1, 1905–DECEMBER 18, 1992
UNITED STATES OF AMERICA

"HOLD THEM, ROCK THEM, LOVE THEM, AND TELL THEM HOW GREAT THEY ARE."
—CLARA HALE

ILLUSTRATION BY
COZBI A. CABRERA

CLARA HOLMES

MODEL

Clara was a bubbly young girl who loved music and dancing, but she was different from the other kids in the neighborhood. Clara was born with a disorder called Ehlers-Danlos syndrome. This illness made her bones weak and caused her constant pain.

Over the years, the illness became worse, and Clara had to start using a wheelchair. She had to plan her activities in advance to be able to manage the pain and to make sure she had time to rest and recover afterward.

Still, Clara went out with friends. She went to the gym, traveled, and always dressed to the nines. Her friends told her she should start a blog to document her style. Clara thought this was a great idea! She named the blog *Rollin Funky*.

One day, two women chased Clara and her boyfriend down the road. *Why are you following us?* they asked. The ladies said they had spotted Clara and her four-inch heels from a nearby coffee shop. They were amazed to see someone so fashionable in a wheelchair. They were scouts from a modeling agency, and they wanted to sign Clara!

She joined the agency and became an instant hit on social media. Soon she was working with fashion brands, fitness brands, watch brands, and more.

Clara uses her platform to promote body positivity and self-love. She is proud to show the world that people with disabilities are just like everyone else, striving to live their best lives every day.

BORN JULY 30, 1980
UNITED KINGDOM

"I THINK IT'S IMPORTANT FOR WOMEN TO CELEBRATE THEIR BODIES AND FEEL COMFORTABLE IN THE SKIN THEY'RE IN."
—CLARA HOLMES

ILLUSTRATION BY
TRUDI-ANN HEMANS

DOMINIQUE JACKSON

ACTOR

Once upon a time, a baby was born on the island of Tobago. The doctors said the child was a boy, but at four years old, Dominique knew she was a girl.

As Dominique got older, the kids in school made fun of her, and people on the island were unkind. Her grandmother was the only person who looked out for her. Tired of being mistreated, Dominique moved to the United States, where the rest of her family lived.

She revealed to her family that she was a woman and that she was going through a process called *transitioning*. She asked them to use the words *her* or *she* when referring to her. Her family did not take the news well. They begged her to keep her transition a secret, but she did not want to hide away. Her mother said, "I will tolerate you, but I will not accept you." Her mother's harsh words broke Dominique's heart.

Rejected by her family, Dominique ended up homeless in New York City. One day, she met a woman who introduced her to ballroom culture. There were competitions called balls where she could dress up in fancy clothes, wear makeup, dance, and strut her stuff without judgment. Finally, she could express herself freely!

In this vibrant scene, Dominique found new opportunities in modeling, acting, and activism. She scored the role of a lifetime in a television show called *Pose*, which explored ballroom culture. Through her character and her advocacy, she educates the world about **transgender** people, showing that they are just like everybody else.

BORN MARCH 20, 1975
TRINIDAD & TOBAGO AND UNITED STATES OF AMERICA

ILLUSTRATION BY
MONET KIFNER

"I STOPPED LOOKING
FOR ACCEPTANCE WHEN
I FOUND MYSELF."
—DOMINIQUE JACKSON

EMILIYA TUREY

HANDBALL PLAYER

Once there was a girl who loved to run fast and throw hard. Her name was Emiliya, and she grew up to be the first Black player on Russia's national handball team.

Emiliya's mother was Russian, and her father was from Sierra Leone. When she traveled for games, people were surprised to see her Russian passport because of the color of her skin. "People don't believe I am Russian," Emiliya said, "although I have lived in Russia all my life."

When she played handball games at home, however, she received love and support from cheering fans.

Before a roaring crowd at the 2007 World Championship finals, Emiliya and six teammates ran into the arena. A fast-paced game, handball is like a mixture of soccer and basketball. Emiliya raced up one side of the court. She caught the ball from her teammate, dribbling after three steps, and aimed to throw it into Norway's goal. She was blocked and knocked onto the floor. Emiliya quickly jumped up, zoomed down the court, and tried to block her opponent, who scored.

Later, she snatched the ball and dashed toward the goal. Jumping into the air, she threw . . . and she scored! That year, Emiliya and her teammates won the gold.

Emiliya triumphed at the World Championship two more times. She also won a silver medal at the 2008 Olympics. By 2013, she'd made 613 goals in 180 games.

Emiliya always gave her best.

BORN OCTOBER 6, 1984
RUSSIA

"WE HAVE TO GIVE
THE BEST WE CAN,
100 PERCENT."
—EMILIYA TUREY

ILLUSTRATION BY
LINDSEY BAILEY

ERIKA "IKA" HÜGEL-MARSHALL

ACTIVIST AND AUTHOR

Ika was born in a small German town. The daughter of a Black American soldier, who left before she was born, and a white German mother, she just wanted to look like everyone else.

After World War II was over, most Germans believed that **mixed-race** children would never fit in with German society. So, at age seven, Ika was taken from her happy home and placed in an orphanage far away.

Because of her skin color, she was often called horrible names. But Ika was stronger than the bullies who tried to make her feel worthless. She thought often of her mother and grandmother, holding on tight to the love they'd shown her.

Ika graduated from college and worked at a children's orphanage. She devoted nine years to transforming the overcrowded center into a loving home. Ika, however, still struggled. She wondered how she could be happy when the white world often rejected her.

In 39 years, she'd never met or seen another Black person. But then she became friends with the Black American poet Audre Lorde and with other Black German writers. She finally found a group where she was accepted as herself. Together, they organized the Afro-German movement, sharing their history and speaking out against **racism** throughout the country. Empowered, Ika wrote her life story, *Invisible Woman: Growing Up Black in Germany*. She finally met her father and was welcomed into her extended US family.

Now a proud Afro-German, Ika never wants to be anything but herself.

BORN MARCH 13, 1947
GERMANY

ILLUSTRATION BY
TEQUITIA ANDREWS

"I'M PROUD TO CALL
MYSELF BLACK,
AFRO-GERMAN,
OR BLACK GERMAN. . . .
NO ONE BUT ME HAS
THE RIGHT TO DEFINE
WHO I AM."
—IKA HÜGEL-MARSHALL

ETHEL JOHNSON, BABS WINGO, AND MARVA SCOTT

WRESTLERS

Ethel was a girl who dreamed of rings—wrestling rings! She watched her older sister, Babs, wrestle at the gym. It looked like so much fun that she decided to try it too! The sisters grew up at a time when few women worked outside the home. But with men off fighting in World War II, new opportunities popped up.

Inspired by the way Jackie Robinson integrated baseball, a clever promoter had an exciting idea! He thought Black women wrestlers could draw a big audience. He was right.

Ethel and Babs joined his troupe. They trained for hours, practicing judo, gymnastics, and wrestling moves like falls and flips. Their younger sister, Marva, joined a few years later.

Around 1950, 16-year-old Ethel became one of the first Black women to be a professional wrestler. Babs was right behind her. Small and feisty, Ethel would jump into the air, twist, and strike her opponent with both feet—a move called the standing dropkick. The sisters competed, often against one another, in packed stadiums all over the world.

Because of **segregation**, the sisters couldn't stay in the same hotels or eat at the same restaurants as white wrestlers. Women weren't even allowed to compete in some states. It wasn't always easy, but Ethel and her sisters paved the way for other gutsy girls to tap into the ring.

ETHEL JOHNSON, MAY 14, 1935–SEPTEMBER 14, 2018
BABS WINGO, CIRCA 1934–APRIL 11, 2003
MARVA SCOTT, NOVEMBER 21, 1937–AUGUST 15, 2003

UNITED STATES OF AMERICA

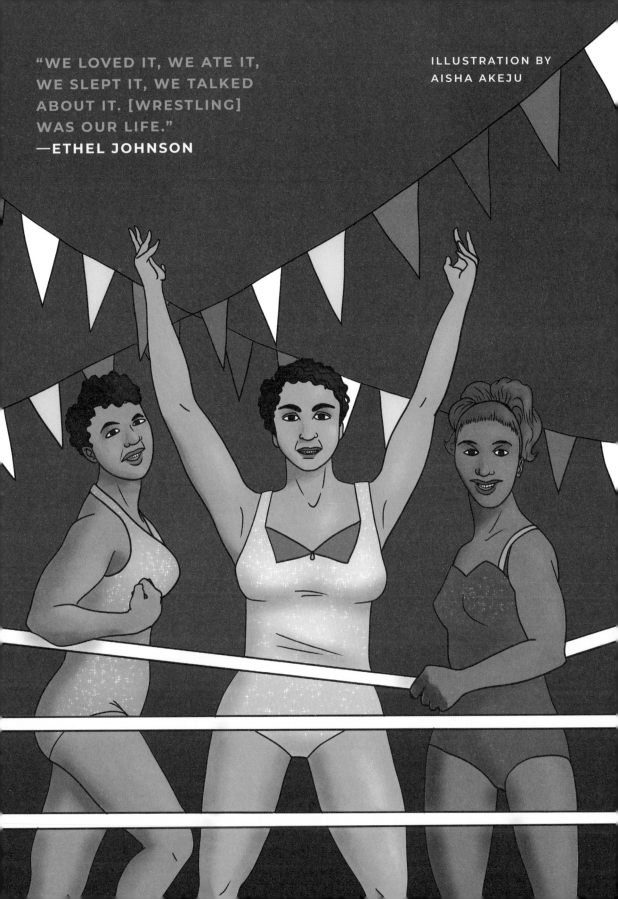

"WE LOVED IT, WE ATE IT, WE SLEPT IT, WE TALKED ABOUT IT. [WRESTLING] WAS OUR LIFE."
—ETHEL JOHNSON

ILLUSTRATION BY AISHA AKEJU

FLO HYMAN

VOLLEYBALL PLAYER

Flo was much taller than her siblings and friends. She had long arms and legs and did not like how thin she was. The kids in school taunted her with names like "Jolly Green Giant." She tried to hide her height, but her mother hated it when she slouched. So Flo took up a sport that fit her long frame: volleyball.

At 6'5", Flo played volleyball throughout high school and college. After three years at the University of Houston, Flo wanted to play for the national team. "You're only young once," she said to herself.

Flo joined the national team and helped them win many medals, including a bronze at the World Cup and a silver at the Olympics. Her signature move, "the flying clutchman," was nearly unstoppable. From close to the net, she'd slam the ball down!

Later, Flo moved to Japan to play in the international league. Fans there loved her! Sadly, one day, while sitting on a bench cheering for her team, she collapsed. She was rushed to the hospital but did not survive.

Flo died from an illness called Marfan syndrome, a condition she didn't even know she had. Her long limbs had caused her heart to work twice as hard to pump blood all around her body.

Before Flo died, few people knew about Marfan syndrome. Her death increased awareness and led others, including her brother, to get tested and treated.

A beloved team player, Flo is remembered for her hard work and mighty moves on the court.

JULY 31, 1954–JANUARY 24, 1986
UNITED STATES OF AMERICA AND JAPAN

ILLUSTRATION BY
MYRIAM CHERY

"TO BE TRUE TO
ONESELF IS THE
ULTIMATE TEST
IN LIFE."
—FLO HYMAN

FLORENCE GRIFFITH JOYNER

SPRINTER

Once there was a girl named Florence with fast legs and big dreams. As she zoomed past in her baby walker, her mom called her Lightning! When asked what she wanted to be, young Florence replied, "Everything."

At seven, Florence began running races. She ran faster than everyone. Later, she set records in high school track. Despite being teased for her bold style, Florence was never afraid to be herself.

Though she was a good student, Florence dropped out of college to help support her family. With help from her coach, she found financial aid, returned to school, and became a track star!

At the 1984 Olympics, Florence won a silver medal. She was proud, but she wanted gold. Determined, she started training harder than ever. After she married runner Al Joyner, people began to call her Flo Jo. And Flo Jo made history at the 1988 Olympic Trials.

It was a windy day in July when she blew past her competitors and broke the world record in the 100-meter dash!

At the Olympics two months later, she became the first American woman to win four medals in a single year.

Spectators marveled at Flo Jo's strong muscles and long stride. She also captivated audiences with her flashy look. She sprinted in colorful, sometimes one-legged bodysuits and sported extra-long nails.

With speed and style, Florence inspired a generation of girls. And her records still stand!

DECEMBER 21, 1959–SEPTEMBER 21, 1998
UNITED STATES OF AMERICA

"DRESS GOOD TO LOOK GOOD.
LOOK GOOD TO FEEL GOOD.
AND FEEL GOOD TO RUN FAST!"
—FLORENCE GRIFFITH JOYNER

ILLUSTRATION BY
ALICIA ROBINSON

FUNMILAYO RANSOME-KUTI

ACTIVIST

Frances Abigail Olufunmilayo lived in a land called Abeokuta, now part of Nigeria. Most girls there could not get an education, but Frances's parents enrolled her in a boys-only high school. She was the first girl to join.

At 19, Frances went to England to finish her studies. When she returned, she asked everyone to use her African name, Funmilayo.

Funmilayo believed women should be empowered and independent. She was the first woman in Nigeria to drive a car. She started a club to teach women how to read, sew, and cook. All types of women joined.

When she learned that the government was treating the women who worked in the market unfairly, she rallied them together to fight for their rights. The club she created became a **union**, and it swelled from a couple hundred women to 20,000! Funmilayo trained union members in secret, disguising meetings as picnics or festivals. Together, thousands of women demanded lower taxes and the right to vote.

Abeokuta was ruled by a local king under a British **colonial** government. Funmilayo and her union marched in front of the king's palace singing and chanting. Finally, after two years, the king gave up his throne, and the government met the women's demands.

Funmilayo then fought for independence from British rule, and her union grew even stronger. She took an executive position in a political party and traveled all over the world, using her quick wit and bold words to advocate for Nigerian women's rights.

OCTOBER 25, 1900–APRIL 13, 1978

NIGERIA

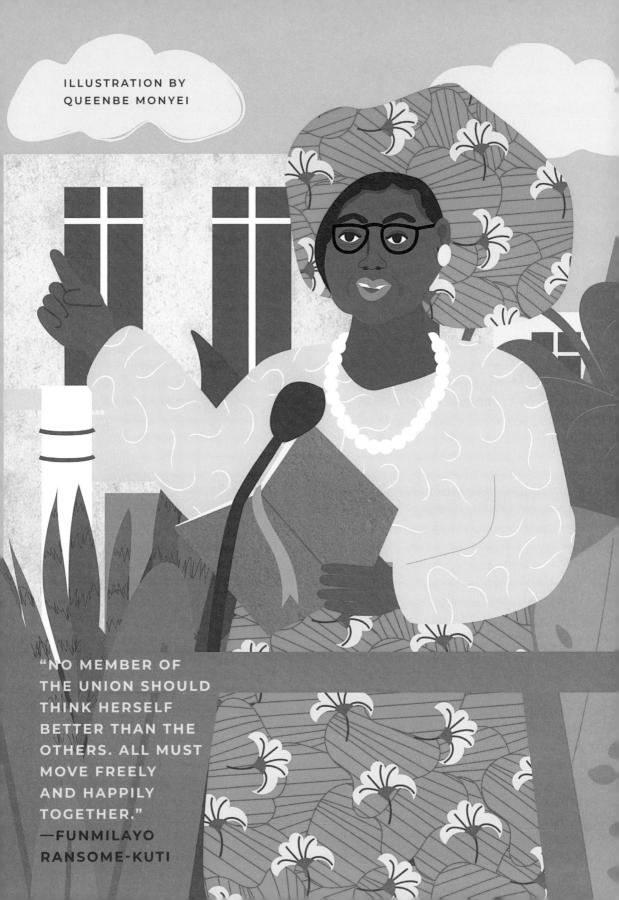

ILLUSTRATION BY
QUEENBE MONYEI

"NO MEMBER OF
THE UNION SHOULD
THINK HERSELF
BETTER THAN THE
OTHERS. ALL MUST
MOVE FREELY
AND HAPPILY
TOGETHER."
—FUNMILAYO
RANSOME-KUTI

GABBY DOUGLAS

GYMNAST

Once there was a girl named Gabby who loved to climb, jump, roll, and tumble. At three, she learned how to do a cartwheel from her older sister. Next were handstands and splits. A year later, she taught herself how to do a one-handed cartwheel!

Gabby started gymnastics training at six. Two years later, she knew what she wanted more than anything: to win at the Olympics.

With long hours at the gym, she suffered many injuries, including a strained hamstring and a split lip. She faced cruel taunts from some racist teammates and even one of her coaches. And at 14, she moved more than 1,000 miles away from home for two years to train with a coach who believed in her. Gabby was terribly homesick. She struggled with self-doubt and wanted to quit. But with the love and support of her family, she pushed past her worries and kept training.

Gabby made it to the 2012 Olympics. Nicknamed the Flying Squirrel, she competed in the all-around events: the vault, uneven bars, balance beam, and floor exercise. With strength and grace, she leaped, flipped, stretched, and spun. Gabby was the first Black gymnast to become an individual all-around champion. She also won a gold in the team competition. The bubbly 16-year-old had achieved her dream!

At the 2016 Olympics, Gabby helped Team USA defend its all-around title, winning another gold medal.

She inspires young people to stay focused and face the hard days "because that's where champions are made."

BORN DECEMBER 31, 1995
UNITED STATES OF AMERICA

ILLUSTRATION BY
ADRIANA BELLET

"I AIM TO DO THE IMPOSSIBLE."
—GABBY DOUGLAS

GLADYS KALEMA-ZIKUSOKA

WILDLIFE VETERINARIAN AND CONSERVATIONIST

When Gladys was a child, she would stay home from school when one of her cats or dogs was sick. In high school, she ran a wildlife club and arranged trips to a national park to see lions, giraffes, and other animals.

Though there were few female animal doctors at the time, Gladys was encouraged by her mother to follow her dreams. At 25, she became Uganda's first wildlife veterinarian.

At the Bwindi Impenetrable National Park, Gladys studied mountain gorillas. She saw that they were similar to humans. Like humans, they lived in family groups, and female gorillas cradled and carried their young. "They're very good mothers," she said. And just like her own children, young gorillas were curious and playful.

But mountain gorillas were at risk of going extinct. There were only about 650 left on Earth. Half of them lived at Bwindi, and Gladys noticed that something was wrong. The gorillas were getting sick with human illnesses. Even though she acted quickly to treat them, one of the baby gorillas at Bwindi died. Heartbroken, Gladys came up with a plan.

She started a nonprofit to work with the villagers near the park to reduce the spread of diseases between humans and gorillas, and the number of endangered mountain gorillas increased to more than 1,000!

Gladys wants humans and mountain gorillas to exist together in health and harmony. So she trains young Ugandans in **conservation** to prevent the extinction of these giant, majestic creatures.

BORN JANUARY 8, 1970
UGANDA

"HELPING ANIMALS
HELPS PEOPLE."
—GLADYS KALEMA-ZIKUSOKA

ILLUSTRATION BY
ALLEANNA HARRIS

IBTIHAJ MUHAMMAD

FENCER

Once there was a girl named Ibtihaj who grew up with five siblings and a commitment to her Muslim faith. She excelled at sports like softball, volleyball, tennis, and track.

Because of their religious beliefs, Ibtihaj's parents wanted her to participate in a sport that allowed her to cover her body and her hair. One day, they suggested she try out for fencing.

She had no idea what fencing was but soon learned it was a sport where participants battle each other using flexible, pointed swords. Fencers wear protective uniforms to keep their bodies safe. Ibtihaj joined her high school fencing team when she was 13 years old.

Ibtihaj was usually one of the only Black girls in her neighborhood. She didn't always feel welcomed at school, and the **hijab** she wore to cover her head made her stand out even more. But her loving parents instilled in her a great sense of self-confidence.

Soon Ibtihaj fell in love with fencing. She trained with all her might and got so good that she competed at the Olympics. There, she made history as the first member of the US team to wear a hijab and the first Muslim American woman to earn a medal.

Suddenly, everyone knew her name! She used her new fame to spread positivity and encourage people to be inclusive—to welcome people who might look, act, or speak differently. She even teamed up with a famous toy maker to release a doll made in her image!

BORN DECEMBER 4, 1985
UNITED STATES OF AMERICA

"I'M HOPING TO CHANGE THE IMAGE THAT PEOPLE MAY HAVE OF MUSLIM WOMEN. WE COME IN ALL DIFFERENT SHAPES, COLORS, AND SIZES, AND WE COME FROM DIFFERENT BACKGROUNDS, AND WE'RE PRODUCTIVE MEMBERS OF SOCIETY."
—IBTIHAJ MUHAMMAD

ILLUSTRATION BY
SANIYYAH ZAHID

IDA B. WELLS

JOURNALIST

When Ida was a baby, the world around her changed in a big way. She was born enslaved in Mississippi. Six months later, the **Emancipation Proclamation** passed. It granted freedom to Black people in the southern United States.

Ida's parents passed away from yellow fever when Ida was 16, and she was left to care for her siblings all by herself. Her parents had made sure she got a good education, so she found a way to support her brothers and sisters. She moved to a nearby city, told everyone she was 18, and became a teacher.

One day, a young Black man Ida knew was killed, along with two of his friends, by a mob of white men. Many other Black men were unjustly killed like this and for the same reason: the color of their skin. The term for these shameful killings is *lynching*.

Ida was outraged. But she didn't just scream and cry. She investigated. Then she published a series of articles in local newspapers and pamphlets. She wanted the world to know what was happening. This was the start of her courageous anti-lynching campaign.

Ida risked her life to travel around the South, investigating and writing about other terrible lynchings. She also went to Washington, DC, and urged the president to take action.

With her courage and moving words, Ida showed girls and women worldwide how to use their leadership and storytelling skills to bring difficult situations to light and advocate for positive change.

JULY 16, 1862–MARCH 25, 1931
UNITED STATES OF AMERICA

"THE WAY TO RIGHT
WRONGS IS TO TURN
THE LIGHT OF TRUTH
UPON THEM."
—IDA B. WELLS

ILLUSTRATION BY
ADRIANA BELLET

IMAN

SUPERMODEL AND BUSINESSWOMAN

When Iman was a little girl in Somalia, war broke out. She and her family were forced to flee to Kenya.

Iman later went to boarding school in Egypt. A clever student, she learned to speak five languages.

Iman grew up to be a tall, graceful woman with striking features. One day, she was walking down the street in Nairobi, where she attended college, when she was stopped by a well-known photographer. He insisted on taking her picture. Iman agreed, knowing that the money she earned would cover her tuition. The pictures changed her life.

Iman moved to New York City, where she modeled for iconic fashion designers. She appeared on runways, in magazines, in movies, and on billboards all over the world!

A few years later, Iman decided to build her own business. She launched a line of cosmetics. Women of color didn't have many makeup options at the time, and her products were a success! With her leadership, IMAN Cosmetics became a multimillion dollar company.

Iman had two children and fell in love with a legendary rock star. But she never forgot where she came from. "I am the face of a **refugee**," she says. She uses her influence to tell people about Somalia—about its widespread beauty as well as its challenges. Her activism has helped raise money to build schools and provide support for vulnerable families in Africa and around the world.

From fashion to foreign affairs, Iman is a fierce force!

BORN JULY 25, 1955
SOMALIA AND UNITED STATES OF AMERICA

"BEAUTY IS BEING
COMFORTABLE AND
CONFIDENT IN YOUR
OWN SKIN."
—IMAN

INSOONI

SINGER

Once, a Korean woman and a Black American soldier had a baby girl named In-soon. When the Korean War ended, In-soon's father went back to the United States. She never saw him again.

In-soon didn't have much to eat, so she hung around the local military bases, perhaps hoping her father would return. The soldiers treated her like a kid sister, sharing their hamburgers and giving her clothes, earrings, and pocket money when they could spare it.

Most of In-soon's classmates had pale skin. They made fun of her, saying her skin was dirty. After middle school, she decided she was done with school and quit so she could put her singing voice to work.

At 21, In-soon joined an all-girl pop group called the Hee Sisters. She sang with them for a while, but her powerful voice always sounded better on its own. So she launched a solo career and started going by the stage name Insooni.

She recorded 19 albums and performed in packed arenas, night clubs, and venues as revered as Carnegie Hall in New York City. When the 2018 Winter Olympics came to South Korea, there was no better choice than Insooni to perform the event's theme song! She sang the cheerful lyrics to "Let Everyone Shine" and encouraged all the athletes to do their best.

Insooni believes her fame comes with responsibility. "Many **biracial** children watch me, so I've got a lot on my shoulders now," she says.

She founded a school to give biracial children an education, free of charge and free from bullying.

BORN APRIL 5, 1957
SOUTH KOREA

"EVERYONE HAS HIS OR HER OWN ORDEAL, LIKE HOW RAIN POURS DOWN ON EVERYONE—BUT THAT'S NOT ETERNAL. THE SKY WILL CLEAR."
—INSOONI

ILLUSTRATION BY TAYLOR MCMANUS

ISSA RAE

ACTOR, WRITER, AND PRODUCER

Once there was a girl named Issa who grew up in the 1990s watching funny stories about Black families on TV. But as she got older, she had a hard time finding shows about Black characters that resembled real life.

Issa fell in love with acting in high school. In college, she created and filmed her own series called *Dorm Diaries*. Students watched and shared it with their friends. Soon college students across the country were hooked!

After college, Issa moved to New York City to pursue her film career. But one night, something awful happened. Thieves broke into her apartment and stole all her filmmaking equipment. They even took the scripts she'd written! Issa was devastated. Later, she sat down, sad and frustrated, and wrote in her journal, "I'm awkward. And Black."

A light bulb went off! Issa realized she could create a comedy series with a fresh perspective, without any of the **stereotypes** she grew up watching. It would be about a girl just like her—young, awkward, and filled with all sorts of thoughts and emotions. Issa wrote and starred in the show and put it on YouTube, and *Awkward Black Girl* became a hit!

Then she worked her magic again, creating a successful show about the friendship between two young Black women—this time for TV.

Issa also started a company to support Black writers and help bring their projects to life. She wants other creators like her to be seen and supported in Hollywood and beyond.

BORN JANUARY 12, 1985
UNITED STATES OF AMERICA

ILLUSTRATION BY
NAOMI SILVERIO

"I LIKE TO CHALLENGE MYSELF.
I LIKE TO OUTDO THE LAST THING I DID."
—ISSA RAE

JACQUELINE DUNKLEY-BENT

MIDWIFE

Once there was a girl named Jacqueline who was happiest when she was helping others. Born to Caribbean parents, she was the youngest of four children. She loved baking with her mom, painting with her dad, and learning karate when her brother practiced on her. Her parents urged her to do her best and try to do what's right.

When Jacqueline grew up, she became a nurse. She enjoyed working with women and babies, so she trained to be a **midwife**. She would help pregnant women during childbirth.

Jacqueline sought out many challenges. She taught at universities, wrote a book on health, and managed the maternity staff for the health care system in the United Kingdom. Then she became England's first chief midwifery officer. In this job, she comes up with ways to improve health care for mothers and their children.

She works to make sure that all women in England—no matter where they live, what their skin color is, or how much money they make— receive the best health care.

Many countries don't have the resources to help keep pregnant women healthy. Sometimes they even die. Jacqueline trains and mentors midwives in West Africa to help prevent these deaths.

Whether she is helping the Duchess of Cambridge deliver Princess Charlotte or a **refugee** mother bring her child into the world, Jacqueline does everything she can to keep mothers and babies safe and strong.

BORN FEBRUARY 20, 1964
UNITED KINGDOM

"MIDWIVES SAVE LIVES."
—JACQUELINE DUNKLEY-BENT

JEANETTE EPPS

ASTRONAUT

Once there was a girl who was a whiz in math and science by the time she was nine years old. Her older brother saw her report card. *You're so smart. you could go to space one day!* he said.

Jeanette earned degrees in **physics** and **aerospace engineering**. And in 2009, the space agency NASA chose her to be an astronaut.

Then the hardest training of her life began. She studied rocks, minerals, and land shapes so she could identify formations like lakes and volcanoes on the surface of the moon. She learned to speak Russian so she could talk to other astronauts. She practiced using ropes to lower herself deep into caves to collect specimens from the slimy walls so she'd be ready to work in any environment. She trained underwater to prepare to walk on the moon, where there is almost no gravity. She operated complex robots and space station technology. She also passed all her exams and physical tests to qualify for a space mission.

NASA planned to send her to live on the International Space Station for six months. Jeanette was thrilled!

Unfortunately, in 2018, right before she was set to blast off, she was pulled from the mission. Another astronaut took her place. NASA never told her why she wasn't allowed to go. Even though she was disappointed, she took the news calmly.

Her friends and family rallied around her. Everyone wanted answers. But Jeanette was willing to wait. She's staying in tip-top shape. When the next opportunity comes, Jeanette will be ready to seize it.

BORN NOVEMBER 3, 1970
UNITED STATES OF AMERICA

"BEING THE FIRST ANYTHING TO ME BEARS A LOT OF RESPONSIBILITY. I'M UP FOR THAT CHALLENGE, BUT AT THE SAME TIME, I'M HOPEFUL."
—JEANETTE EPPS

ILLUSTRATION BY
ALLEANNA HARRIS

J. EPPS

JESSAMYN STANLEY

YOGA TEACHER

Once there was a girl named Jessamyn who was told she was too slow and uncoordinated for team sports.

She decided to try a solo activity instead. She signed up for a yoga class. Jessamyn was excited at first, but when she walked into the room, she noticed her body was bigger and her skin color was darker than everyone else's. Even worse, the class was "hot yoga." The room was set to 105 degrees! Sweaty and frustrated by how hard it was to bend, stretch, and balance in poses she'd never seen before, she gave up and left.

Years later, when Jessamyn was in graduate school, a friend invited her to a yoga class. "Absolutely not," Jessamyn said. She was certain yoga was not for her.

But her friend pushed her to get out of her comfort zone. This time, Jessamyn loved it! Many of the poses were still challenging for her, but she made it to the end of the class and felt proud.

From that day on, Jessamyn stopped saying she couldn't do difficult things. Instead, she told herself she was strong and powerful! Practicing yoga with this positive outlook helped her embrace her body and feel more confident.

Jessamyn studied yoga for years and mastered the poses she once found difficult. She became a nurturing teacher who encourages people of every background and body shape to try yoga.

BORN JUNE 27, 1987
UNITED STATES OF AMERICA

"PUSH YOURSELF TO
THINK BEYOND THE
LIMITS OTHERS PLACE ON
YOU. LOOK WITHIN AND
UNDERSTAND THAT YOU
ARE ENOUGH JUST AS
YOU ARE."
—JESSAMYN STANLEY

ILLUSTRATION BY
ALEXANDRA BOWMAN

JOY BUOLAMWINI

COMPUTER SCIENTIST

Growing up in Mississippi, Joy said she "saw art and science as one." She spent time in her father's computer lab and became interested in robots. She wanted to learn how they worked, so she taught herself how to design websites and write computer code.

While in college studying computer science, Joy realized there was a problem with the technology used to make robots. A robot could recognize her roommate's light-skinned face but not hers. A year later, on a school trip to Hong Kong, Joy tested some more robots. Again, they did not recognize her dark-skinned face.

Joy shrugged and thought, *Maybe one day someone will notice this and fix it.*

While getting her master's degree, Joy worked as a researcher on a project that used technology to identify faces. Once again, the system did not detect her face. But when she tested the tech on a Black man's face, it worked. Curious, Joy put on a white mask and tested the system again. Her face, now covered by the mask, was recognizable. It became clear to Joy that the technology noticed white faces and Black male faces, but not Black female faces.

Joy knew that if she said nothing, Black women everywhere would be misidentified by computers. She spoke up to pressure companies like Microsoft and Google to fix their facial recognition programs. By calling them out, she became a digital activist, fighting for proper representation of Black women in new technology.

BORN JANUARY 23, 1990

CANADA, GHANA, AND UNITED STATES OF AMERICA

"I INVITE YOU TO JOIN ME IN
CREATING A WORLD WHERE
TECHNOLOGY WORKS FOR
ALL OF US, NOT JUST SOME OF US."
—JOY BUOLAMWINI

JOY HARDEN BRADFORD

PSYCHOLOGIST

Joy was an amazing listener. Friends always went to her with their problems. Because of her gift, Joy decided to go to school for **psychology** to study human behavior. In 2006, she became Dr. Joy.

At first, she started helping people one by one in therapy sessions. Her clients would share their stories, and she did what she did best: she listened. "Therapy is a great space to help you work through some patterns in your life," she said.

Dr. Joy started to notice a few problems: Many people thought therapy was just for people who were "crazy." Black women often found it hard to admit they needed help. And there weren't enough Black women therapists.

She knew just what to do. She created a directory called Therapy for Black Girls to help Black women easily find the health care they need. Her list started out with just 90 therapists. A few years later, it had grown to more than 1,400 doctors and counselors from all over the country.

Dr. Joy also wanted everyone to know that seeing a doctor and asking for help was totally normal! She started a podcast where she talks about dealing with anxiety and depression, practicing self-care, and other topics. In some episodes, Dr. Joy even held pretend sessions with popular TV characters to show that therapy wasn't scary at all.

Dr. Joy is dedicated to making sure all Black women and girls have access to the care they need to keep their minds healthy.

BORN 1979

UNITED STATES OF AMERICA

"THERAPY HELPS YOU BETTER UNDERSTAND HOW YOU SHOW UP IN THE WORLD. . . . THERAPY CAN ACT AS A MIRROR TO HELP YOU SEE YOURSELF TRULY."
—JOY HARDEN BRADFORD

ILLUSTRATION BY
GABRIELLE FLUDD

JOY REID

JOURNALIST AND TV NEWS HOST

In Joy's family, adventures weren't just for the adults. Once, while Joy's mother was writing a book, she packed up the family and drove them from Colorado to Mexico. They spent the summer there, experiencing exciting new things. Joy adored her mother, who was an immigrant from a small country in South America called British Guiana. From her, Joy learned to be independent, proud, and adventurous.

At 17, she was accepted to Harvard University, where she planned to study medicine. Sadly, just weeks before school started, her mother died of breast cancer. Joy took a year off from school to grieve. Then she decided to pursue her interest in film and storytelling.

After college, Joy got married, moved to Florida with her three children, and began her career as a journalist. As a newspaper columnist, she covered the story of Travyon Martin, an innocent Black boy, who was killed by a neighborhood patrol guard. His death sparked outrage across the nation. Joy's detailed and descriptive reporting impressed viewers and producers alike. Soon she was hosting her own TV show. And in 2020, Joy made history as the first Black woman to host a nightly news show!

She always appears on the news as her most authentic self, often rocking natural hairstyles to help empower other Black women.

Joy believes that picturing your goals helps you reach them. "There's a saying that you should 'speak it into existence,'" she said. "I say 'write it into existence.'" Many of her dreams have already come true, and Joy continues to live fearlessly—just like her mother taught her!

BORN DECEMBER 8, 1968
UNITED STATES OF AMERICA

ILLUSTRATION BY
ELIZABETH MONTERO SANTA

"DON'T BE AFRAID TO
RAISE YOUR HAND,
BUT ONCE YOU DO,
MAKE SURE YOU'RE
PREPARED—BECAUSE
WHEN IT'S TIME FOR
YOU TO SHINE, YOU
WILL SHINE."
—JOY REID

JUDITH JAMISON

DANCER AND CHOREOGRAPHER

Judith could never stay put. She was always jumping and playing. She even crashed her first bicycle straight into a tree!

To help Judith work out some of her wiggly energy, her mother put her in ballet lessons when she was six. Judith was a natural.

She danced all through elementary school and high school and right into college, moving her body through the steps and rhythms of many styles of dance, from cultures around the world. She tried them all.

One day, she attended a performance of the Alvin Ailey American Dance Theater. Sitting in the audience watching the fluid movements of the dancers, Judith thought, *I can do that.*

She decided to audition, but it did not go well. She felt clunky, unsure, and stiff. The free-flowing routines combined with the jazzy music were so different from the ballet she knew. She left the audition in tears.

But she had underestimated her talent. Three days later, Judith was invited to join the dance company. In time, she mastered modern dance and performed all over the world.

Judith dabbled in Broadway plays, choreographed performances, and started her own dance company. And when Alvin Ailey died in 1989, she was asked back. She became the first Black woman to direct a modern dance company. Even after her retirement—and even when her bones felt achy—Judith admitted that she couldn't sit still. "I've been in extraordinary motion my entire life," she says.

BORN MAY 10, 1943

UNITED STATES OF AMERICA

ILLUSTRATION BY
RENIKE

"DANCE FROM THE
TOP OF YOUR HEAD TO
THE BOTTOM OF YOUR
FEET. . . . EVEN WHEN
YOU'RE STATIONARY,
YOU MUST BE MOVING
AND ALIVE."
—JUDITH JAMISON

JULIA LÓPEZ

PAINTER

Little Julia didn't own a single paintbrush, but she grew up and taught herself to paint. As a child, she worked on her parents' farm in Mexico, gathering crops to sell with her siblings. They used the money to visit local fairs. There, Julia saw photographs of faraway places she wanted to visit.

One night, while everyone slept, she decided to leave her life of labor behind. At 13 years old, Julia ran away. Her family scooped her up and brought her home. But later, she made her way to Mexico City, a bustling place 300 miles from her home. Julia found her godmother and worked as a maid. Many residents were fascinated by her beauty because of her mixed **heritage**—Chilean, African, and indigenous Amuzgo.

Later, she met the famous painter Frida Kahlo, who helped her get a job posing for artists. As Julia modeled, she watched the painters work. Suddenly, she wanted to paint too.

Julia used paper bags as canvases. She created landscapes using vivid emerald greens and peacock blues. Every painting showed scenes from her childhood in the countryside, like horses standing by a tree-lined river or dark-skinned girls holding flowers. Excited, she shared her work with a teacher at the school. He pushed her to keep painting but refused to teach her. "Why?" Julia asked. He said he didn't want her to lose her unique style.

At her first exhibit, in 1955, her work sold for just 20 cents apiece. But soon, she was celebrated for painting the rural farm life she'd left behind.

BORN 1936
MEXICO

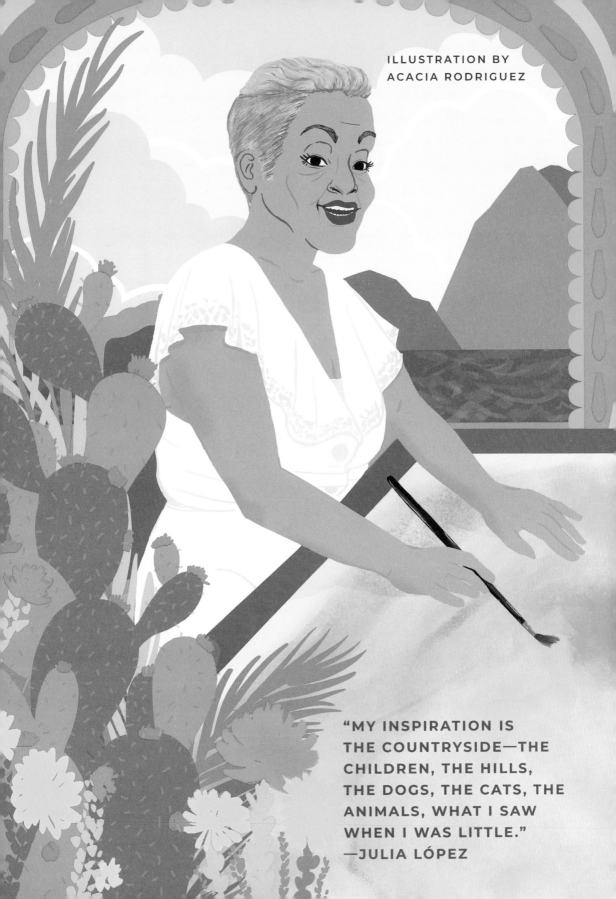

ILLUSTRATION BY
ACACIA RODRIGUEZ

"MY INSPIRATION IS
THE COUNTRYSIDE—THE
CHILDREN, THE HILLS,
THE DOGS, THE CATS, THE
ANIMALS, WHAT I SAW
WHEN I WAS LITTLE."
—JULIA LÓPEZ

KAMALA HARRIS

VICE PRESIDENT

Once upon a time, there was a girl who attended civil rights marches before she was even born. Later, her parents, who were originally from India and Jamaica, took her to protests where they shouted chants while wide-eyed Kamala watched from her stroller.

Eventually, Kamala outgrew the stroller and ventured onto the streets of Oakland, California, on her own. She knew she wanted to be someone who could help others in times of trouble.

At Howard University, in Washington, DC, she followed in the footsteps of many famous Black lawyers who came before her.

During an internship on Capitol Hill, she walked by the Supreme Court building every day. On it, the words "Equal Justice Under Law" are etched into the stone. Kamala thought about how to make sure those words were true for everybody.

She became a lawyer, asking tough questions and battling fierce adversaries with her words. Kamala demanded that people listen to her.

She ran for office and became the first-ever female district attorney in the San Francisco Bay Area, beating out her old boss for the job. She later ran for attorney general of the whole state of California—and won!

Then Kamala climbed even higher. She was elected to the United States Senate. And in 2020, former vice president Joe Biden chose her as his running mate when he ran for president. The powerful pair won the election, and Kamala became the first woman, first Black person, and first South Asian person to ever hold that office.

BORN OCTOBER 20, 1964
UNITED STATES OF AMERICA

ILLUSTRATION BY
NICOLE MILES

"WHILE I MAY BE THE
FIRST WOMAN IN THIS
OFFICE, I WON'T BE
THE LAST."
—KAMALA HARRIS

KHERIS ROGERS

FASHION DESIGNER

Kheris always had glowing dark brown skin and a sense of style. But at her school in Los Angeles, she stood out. She was one of only four Black students.

Once, while drawing, Kheris looked for a color to fill in her skin. The teacher handed her a crayon that was black as coal. It didn't resemble her skin tone at all!

Kheris came home in tears and told her sister, Taylor, all about it. Taylor reminded Kheris that their grandmother always told them to "flex in their **complexion**." Kheris didn't know what that meant exactly.

Taylor dressed her sister in pretty clothes and asked her to pose. She took photos and posted them online with the tagline "Flexin' in Her Complexion." The internet went wild! Uplifting comments poured in.

Kheris wanted to help as many people as possible feel comfortable in their skin. She decided to print T-shirts with her family slogan and sell them online. Her mom donated $100 so Kheris could start her business, and the first batch of shirts sold out within minutes!

Celebrities took notice, sporting Kheris's shirts in their social media posts. Soon she appeared in fashion events, TV shows, and ads.

"Flexin' in My Complexion means to me that you are beautiful," Kheris said. "Beauty has nothing to do with the outside. It has to do with your inside by being nice, smart, creative. Being beautiful means confidently knowing that you're enough just the way you are."

BORN AUGUST 6, 2006
UNITED STATES OF AMERICA

KIMBERLY BRYANT

ENGINEER AND ENTREPRENEUR

O nce there was a girl whose head was filled with numbers. Growing up, Kimberly was fascinated by technology and had a deep interest in math and science. After high school, she went to a prestigious university, where she studied electrical engineering.

Kimberly took her first computer programming class as a freshman and loved it. She couldn't believe all the incredible things computers could do. The possibilities were endless!

But as much as technology excited her, Kimberly was sad to see that there were few Black girls in her classes. Her computer engineering classes were filled with white men.

Still, she pursued a career in technology. She also became a mother. One day, her daughter, Kai, said she wanted to learn computer programming. Kimberly looked for classes for her. Unfortunately, all the courses she found were tailored to boys. Kimberly didn't want her daughter to face the same feeling of isolation that she had experienced.

Kimberly had an idea! In 2011, she founded Black Girls Code, an organization dedicated to teaching young Black girls lessons in science, technology, engineering, and math.

Kimberly's goal is to increase the number of opportunities available to women and girls in technology and to teach them the skills they need to thrive. She plans to change the lives of one million Black girls by 2040. And she is well on her way!

BORN JANUARY 14, 1967
UNITED STATES OF AMERICA

"YOU CAN ABSOLUTELY BE WHAT YOU CAN'T SEE! THAT'S WHAT INNOVATORS AND DISRUPTERS DO."
—KIMBERLY BRYANT

ILLUSTRATION BY OCTAVIA JACKSON

KRISTAL AMBROSE

ENVIRONMENTALIST

Once there lived a girl in the Bahamas who swam in the sea every day. She loved the way the cool water felt against her skin, and she loved laughing and playing in the sand with her siblings.

What lies beneath the surface of the sea? Kristal wondered. At a young age, she knew she wanted to become a marine scientist.

Working at an aquarium as a teenager changed her life. One day, Kristal was asked to help a sea turtle that had swallowed plastic. It broke her heart to see an animal suffering because of pollution in the ocean. Kristal made a promise. She would never drop plastic on the ground again. And she would do everything she could to help keep the oceans clean and sea creatures safe.

But everywhere she looked, she saw water bottles, jugs, and torn plastic bags in jumbled heaps, tangled with seaweeds and trash. Litter piled up on beaches that should have been covered with scuttling crabs, skittering shorebirds, and playing children instead.

Kristal launched the Bahamas Plastic Movement to help remove the plastic waste. She also started a free summer camp where kids can learn about marine life and what they can do to protect it.

Kristal and her students drafted a bill banning single-use plastics in the Bahamas. "We are the change. We are the solution. We can fix this plastic pollution!" they chanted as they addressed the government.

In 2018, the bill passed! One ocean-loving young woman harnessed her power, lifted her voice, and protected the shores she loved so much.

BORN DECEMBER 7, 1989
THE BAHAMAS

"I CAN HARNESS THE ENERGY OF THE SEA."
—KRISTAL AMBROSE

ILLUSTRATION BY
KETURAH ARIEL

LADI KWALI

POTTER

In the country of Nigeria, there lived a girl who loved pottery. Ladi came from a gifted family that made pots for cooking and storing water, as well as decoration.

Ladi was young when her aunt taught her to make pottery. She learned fast and was especially good at the pinching and coiling method. She'd place the pot on a stool and mold it while walking around it. Round and round she'd go, adding strips of clay, then smoothing it to a solid finish.

People loved the patterns of birds, fish, lizards, and scorpions that Ladi etched from her imagination. Her work was so popular that she often sold all her pots before she could even get them to the market.

A government official was astonished by the amount of detail in Ladi's work and invited her to join a pottery training center he'd established.

At the center, Ladi further developed her talent by learning wheel throwing, glazing, and using a clay oven called a kiln to harden and dry pots. She made teapots, jugs, bowls, plates, and cups. She was the first female potter to train there and soon became an instructor.

Ladi was new to the modern way of pottery but still mastered it to perfection. She enjoyed mixing traditional and modern methods, particularly when making decorative pots. With a modern touch, her products rose in price and demand. Everyone wanted a polished Ladi Kwali piece in their home! Her reputation quickly spread across continents.

CIRCA 1925–AUGUST 12, 1984

NIGERIA

LEAH CHASE

CHEF

Leah's family may have been poor, but they ate like royalty. They had okra, sweet potatoes, and chicken from her father's farm.

At the time, schools were segregated. And since there wasn't a Black high school nearby, Leah moved to her aunt's home in New Orleans.

There, she met and married a trumpet player nicknamed Dooky. His parents owned a sandwich shop. When his father got sick, Dooky and Leah helped out and later took over the beloved neighborhood hotspot.

Over time, Dooky Chase's restaurant became the only fine dining spot for the Black community in New Orleans. It was also a place where people planned for a better world. Civil rights leaders met there to discuss strategy over meals with white allies even though it was illegal for Black and white people to mix. Leah also fed musicians, actors, and even presidents alongside the local community.

Leah was Creole, a term referring to Louisiana's **mixed-race** population—French, Spanish, African, and Native American—and she served up Creole favorites like gumbo. In large pots, she simmered this rich, flavorful stew filled with sausage, shrimp, crab, chicken, and beef and earthy flavors like onion, garlic, and parsley.

After her first visit to a museum, Leah was inspired. She wanted to provide her customers with more than delicious food. Soon the walls of her restaurant were covered with vibrant art by Black artists.

The Queen of Creole Cuisine served her community seven days a week. Today, her children and grandchildren keep up the tradition.

JANUARY 6, 1923–JUNE 1, 2019
UNITED STATES OF AMERICA

"IN MY DINING ROOM, WE CHANGED THE COURSE OF AMERICA OVER A BOWL OF GUMBO AND SOME FRIED CHICKEN."
—LEAH CHASE

Dooky Chase's

ILLUSTRATION BY NICOLE MILES

LÉOPOLDINE DOUALLA-BELL SMITH

FLIGHT ATTENDANT

Once there was a princess who made history in the sky. Her name was Léopoldine, of the royal Douala family of Cameroon. She loved animals and wanted to be a veterinarian. But her father said women could only be nurses or teachers. Her father was wrong.

While in high school, Léopoldine got a job at an international airline terminal. She assisted passengers who arrived from all over the world, welcoming them to Cameroon.

After graduating, she trained to be a flight attendant. But just before her very first flight, she panicked. She had never been on a plane before! At 17 years old, Léopoldine did not realize she was breaking boundaries as the first Black flight attendant.

Many African countries were becoming independent, and Léopoldine had a front-row seat to a changing Africa.

Some passengers pouted and protested at the idea of a Black woman serving them, touching their bags, or just being in their presence. Léopoldine ignored their **racism**. She would simply smile and walk away. One day, she landed in South Africa and was not even allowed to walk off the plane with her white colleagues.

Despite the challenges she faced, Léopoldine kept opening doors for other women in the travel industry. Now retired and living in the United States, she still volunteers. In her white cowboy hat, she welcomes visitors to the airport with a bright smile.

BORN 1939
CAMEROON

"MY SIBLINGS AND I WERE RAISED TO WELCOME FOREIGNERS AND TO MAKE THEM FEEL AT HOME IN OUR PART OF AFRICA. THAT IS THE REASON I WAS OPEN TO CULTURES."
—LÉOPOLDINE DOUALLA-BELL SMITH

ILLUSTRATION BY SARAH LOULENDO

LISA LESLIE

BASKETBALL PLAYER

Once there was a left-handed girl named Lisa who was taller than her second-grade teacher. Kids called her names, but her mother encouraged her to be proud of her height.

Everyone asked Lisa if she played basketball. She hated that question. But she wanted to fit in, so she decided to try it out. Soon she learned to dribble and shoot right-handed like everyone else. Lisa kept training and became so good that more than 100 colleges reached out to her—even before she started high school!

The key to becoming a champion, she said, was setting goals. She wrote down her objectives and pinned them all over the house.

After thriving on the college courts, Lisa set her sights on the Olympics. Sadly, opportunities for women were limited. Men could play in the National Basketball Association (NBA). But there wasn't a US women's league yet. So Lisa played in Italy before earning her spot on the US Olympic team. In 1996, she won a gold medal at her first Olympic Games!

That same year, the NBA created a women's league, the WNBA, and Lisa joined the LA Sparks in 1997. Five years later, in front of cheering fans, Lisa caught a long pass and charged toward the basket. The announcer cried, "What is she going to do?" Just then, she made history as the first woman at a WNBA game to slam-dunk!

She won three most valuable player awards and three more Olympic gold medals. Then, after 12 seasons, Lisa retired from basketball. She finished her business degree and returned to the Sparks as an owner.

BORN JULY 7, 1972
UNITED STATES OF AMERICA

"I WANT TO PROVE ONCE AGAIN, TO EVERY LITTLE GIRL OR BOY THAT HAS GOALS AND WORKS HARD, THAT THEY CAN DO AND ACHIEVE ANYTHING. ABSOLUTELY ANYTHING."
—LISA LESLIE

ILLUSTRATION BY
KIM HOLT

MC SOFFIA

RAPPER

Soffia never wanted to be a princess. She always dreamed of being a hero instead. Her skin was black. Her hair was coily. And her greatest power was her voice. With it, she sent a very important message: may Black girls love and accept themselves and each other.

When Soffia was just five years old, her classmates began bullying her because of her dark skin. One of them told her she was so dark because she'd fallen into a can of paint as a baby. Those words hurt.

"I want to be white," Soffia told her mother.

Kamilah, her mom, was outraged. She thought being Black was beautiful and powerful. There was absolutely nothing wrong with her dark skin. So Kamilah began teaching Soffia to celebrate her **heritage**.

Soffia went to her first hip-hop workshop at six, and her rap career began at seven. She worked on lyrics that would later be recorded in a real studio.

In 2016, she released her first music video, "Menina Pretinha," which means "little Black girl" in Portuguese. In it, 12-year-old Soffia sang: "I'm Black, and I'm proud of my color."

That same year, Soffia performed with the most famous female rapper in Brazil, Karol Conká, during the opening ceremony of the Olympics. Backstage, Soffia was nervous. But when she held the cold microphone in her hand, she knew she was ready. She stepped onto the enormous stage, and her words flowed out with confidence and power.

BORN FEBRUARY 22, 2004
BRAZIL

ILLUSTRATION BY
KEISHA OKAFOR

"I'LL BE REPRESENTING ALL
THE BLACK KIDS FROM THE
OUTSKIRTS WHO CAN'T BE
HEARD. I'LL BE THEIR VOICE."
—MC SOFFIA

MAMIE PHIPPS CLARK

PSYCHOLOGIST

There once was a Black girl named Mamie who grew up in the segregated South. She earned her **psychology** degree and later became the first Black woman to earn her PhD at Columbia University.

Always interested in working with kids, Mamie studied how **racism** influenced Black children's self-esteem. Fascinated by her research, her husband, Kenneth, joined in.

They conducted a study called the "doll test." Black children were presented with two dolls, one Black and one white. They would ask questions like, "Which doll do you like best?" or "Which doll is nice?"

They discovered that most of the Black children from segregated areas rejected the Black doll and more often described the white doll as "nice." Because these children didn't go to school with white kids, Mamie said they could never learn that they were just as good and just as bright as white students.

Mamie and Kenneth's eye-opening research helped lead to the US Supreme Court's **unanimous** decision in *Brown v. Board of Education*, which ended **segregation** in public schools!

Mamie also founded the first center to provide therapy for children in Harlem, a bustling Black neighborhood in New York City. There, she fought alongside families whose children were not getting the education they were entitled to in the public schools.

Mamie knew that Black children were just as smart and creative as white children, and she wanted to be sure they knew it too.

APRIL 18, 1917–AUGUST 11, 1983
UNITED STATES OF AMERICA

"LET US MAKE NO MISTAKE HERE: RACISM IS A DISEASE."
—MAMIE PHIPPS CLARK

ILLUSTRATION BY
OCTAVIA JACKSON

MARGARET BUSBY

PUBLISHER

Wherever Margaret looked, there were only books by white authors about white people. In school, her teachers never assigned books by Black writers. She knew she had to change that.

One night, she went to a book release party in the London garden where *Peter Pan* had been written. With what seemed like magic in the air, she met a man named Clive Allison. They discussed their love of literature for hours and decided to go into business together.

In 1967, the Allison & Busby publishing house was born.

At first, the pair kept their day jobs. They worked on books in the evenings and on weekends. They sold their first books door to door and on the street. "Would you like to buy a poetry book?" they would ask.

Their method wasn't very successful. Eventually, they found a distributor to help get their books into more hands.

Over the years, Margaret and Clive found, edited, and published poetry, short stories, novels, and science fiction by overlooked writers. They rescued old books and breathed new life into them.

In 1992, Margaret collected the poetry, essays, and political writings of more than 200 Black women in a book called *Daughters of Africa*. It was so successful that she published another collection in 2019. "May all who find their way to this anthology," she wrote, "regardless of gender, class, or race, feast well on its banquet of words."

The first Black female publisher in the United Kingdom, Margaret increased the **diversity** in literature one story at a time.

OCTOBER 11, 1944

GHANA AND UNITED KINGDOM

ILLUSTRATION BY
NICOLE MILES

"WRITE BECAUSE YOU
REALLY ENJOY IT, AND
LEARN TO BE A GOOD
READER BECAUSE THE
BEST WRITERS READ
VORACIOUSLY."
—MARGARET BUSBY

MARÍA ISABEL URRUTIA

WEIGHTLIFTER

When María was just 13 years old, she competed in shot put, a sport that involved throwing a heavy metal ball as far as she could. She won many competitions in South America. Though María's father complained that the sport was too dangerous for a girl, she continued to compete.

As a young woman, she worked as a phone operator to help pay for her training. She woke up at four a.m. every day to go to work. Then she trained in the afternoon and went to school in the evening.

In 1988, María represented Colombia at the Summer Olympics in Seoul, South Korea. She did not win a medal, but while there, she met a Bulgarian trainer who had a great idea. He convinced her to try a new sport: weightlifting.

After just three months of weightlifting, María competed at the world championships in Manchester, England, and won the silver medal! She was so skilled that she won nine more medals after that.

Sadly, her government didn't offer her much support. She needed equipment to get stronger but could not get any. Feeling defeated, she decided to retire from the sport. Just then, the Olympic committee added women's weightlifting to the 2000 Olympic Games. *Maybe just one more competition*, she thought . . . and she won!

María was the first Colombian to win an Olympic gold medal. After her victory, she retired, became a politician, and did her best to help her fellow athletes get the support they needed to succeed.

BORN MARCH 25, 1965
COLOMBIA

ILLUSTRATION BY
MIA SAINE

"THIS WIN IS FOR THOSE
WHO BELIEVED IN ME AND
THOSE WHO DIDN'T."
—MARÍA ISABEL URRUTIA

MARSAI MARTIN

ACTOR AND EXECUTIVE PRODUCER

Once there was a girl named Marsai who dreamed of becoming a superstar. When people asked her, "What do you want to be when you grow up?" she would say, "A legend!"

Marsai was an only child. She spent a lot of time entertaining herself and her parents by putting on skits and performances in her family's living room.

One day, she went to the mall with her family and had her portrait taken. The photographer was impressed with how well she took direction and how she shone on camera. He persuaded her family to submit the pictures to an agency. Soon enough, agents began scrambling to sign her. Marsai landed her first national commercial, and in 2013, her family moved to Los Angeles to pursue her acting career.

When she was 10 years old, Marsai auditioned for a role on the TV show *Black-ish*, about the experiences of a modern-day Black family in the United States. It catapulted her to fame!

Marsai didn't just want to star in movies—she wanted to make them too. So she launched a company with her parents called Genius Productions. She had an idea for an empowering movie with a cast of all Black women. She pitched the idea to movie executives, and they loved it. At just 13 years old, she became the youngest **executive producer** in Hollywood history! She was cast in the lead role, and the film, *Little*, was a big success.

Young Marsai's childhood wish came true—she's a real-life legend!

BORN AUGUST 21, 2004
UNITED STATES OF AMERICA

ILLUSTRATION BY
KEISHA OKAFOR

"GO GET YOUR YES."
—MARSAI MARTIN

MARSHA P. JOHNSON

ACTIVIST

Once there was a child who helped start a movement. Though the doctors said the child was a boy at birth, the little one always knew that a boy name and boy clothes felt wrong. At age five, Marsha put on a dress. She felt good and thought she looked good too.

Bullies at school didn't think so, though. Marsha didn't get to wear another dress until after high school graduation.

She moved to New York City with $15 and a bag of clothes. Marsha didn't know anybody yet and ended up living on the street. New York was loud and scary, with its honking cars and massive buildings. But Marsha found a home in Greenwich Village on Christopher Street.

Soon everybody seemed to know her. They called her "Queen" and "Saint." She strolled the streets wearing bright colors, sequins, and glitter. She tucked fake fruit and flowers into her hair. But New York City was far from paradise, especially for LGBTQIA+ people.

On June 28, 1969, the police raided the Stonewall Inn, a local club in Marsha's neighborhood where LGBTQIA+ people gathered. But the people fought back. They turned over cars and set things on fire. Marsha shouted and resisted arrest. She was not alone.

That night, the Stonewall Riots began, sparking the LGBTQIA+ rights movement. Afterward, Marsha and her friend Sylvia Rivera started an organization that took care of homeless **transgender** kids. They provided food, clothes, shelter, and a loving community. Marsha opened her big heart to make sure that others wouldn't suffer like she had.

AUGUST 24, 1945–JULY 6, 1992
UNITED STATES OF AMERICA

ILLUSTRATION BY NAKI NARH

"HOW MANY YEARS HAS IT TAKEN PEOPLE TO REALIZE WE ARE ALL BROTHERS AND SISTERS AND HUMAN BEINGS IN THE HUMAN RACE?"
—MARSHA P. JOHNSON

MEGHAN MARKLE

DUCHESS OF SUSSEX AND HUMANITARIAN

Once there was a girl named Meghan who grew up to be a duchess! The daughter of a Black mother and a white father, she always believed in equality.

When she was 11, her class was watching TV. A dish soap commercial came on, and a man's voice said, "Women are fighting greasy pots and pans . . ."

Laughing, two boys agreed that women belonged in the kitchen.

Hurt and angry, Meghan had to do something. Her dad encouraged her to write letters to the most influential people she could think of. She wrote to the company that made the soap, a women's rights lawyer, and US First Lady Hillary Clinton. Three months later, the company changed the word *women* in the ad to *people*. Meghan was amazed! She'd made a difference by speaking up for her beliefs.

While pursuing an acting career, Meghan kept raising her voice for change. In a moving speech, she reminded listeners that it wasn't enough to believe in equality—they must work at it too. After learning that millions of girls don't get an education because of shame around getting their periods, she wrote an article about it in *Time* magazine.

In 2018, Meghan married Prince Harry of the British royal family and became a princess. Her title is the Duchess of Sussex.

Meghan believes it will take all people—girls and women, boys and men, people of all skin colors—working together to build a more **equitable** world.

BORN AUGUST 4, 1981
UNITED STATES OF AMERICA AND UNITED KINGDOM

"EQUALITY DOES NOT PUT ANYONE ON THE BACK FOOT. IT PUTS US ALL ON THE SAME FOOTING, WHICH IS A FUNDAMENTAL HUMAN RIGHT."
—MEGHAN MARKLE

ILLUSTRATION BY
DATA ORUWARI

MURIEL TRAMIS

VIDEO GAME DESIGNER

Once upon a time there was a girl named Muriel who loved to play games of all kinds: crossword puzzles, board games, riddles, cards, logic problems, and more.

Eventually, she started making up her own. She came up with exciting scenarios, stories, characters, and rules. It was much more satisfying than playing games invented by other people! She enjoyed watching the delight on her friends' faces when they played her games.

At 16, Muriel left Martinique, her home island in the Caribbean Sea, to study engineering in Paris. Her first job was programming drones for the French army, but Muriel didn't want her work to be used in war.

She left that job and joined a new company. This team made video games, and they loved her ideas! She experimented with mixing history, folktales, and supernatural stories in her games.

In 1987, Muriel's first game, *Mewilo*, came out. A year later, her second game, *Freedom: Rebels in the Darkness*, was released. Both games were adventures set in Martinique during slavery.

Not all of Muriel's creations were historical. She worked on games about goblins, quests, daring adventures, and even educational topics, like math and science, to encourage girls like her to pursue scientific and technical paths.

Muriel was surprised to find out later in her career that she's known as the first Black woman in video gaming. She hopes many more game-loving girls will join her!

BORN SEPTEMBER 16, 1958
MARTINIQUE AND FRANCE

NANDI BUSHELL

DRUMMER

Once there was a girl who spread joy and happiness one beat at a time. Nandi was born in Durban, South Africa, and her family moved to England when she was two years old.

When Nandi was five, her father would play music from the British rock band the Beatles while making her pancakes. One member of the band, Ringo Starr, caught Nandi's attention. She marveled at how well he played the drums.

Her parents said she could have a drum set only if she did well in school. So she did her schoolwork and brought home excellent grades.

Nandi's father started teaching her how to play her new drums. She practiced every day, and soon enough, she was playing better than him! Nandi loved rock music and could copy the exact rhythm of all her favorite songs.

Her parents saw how talented she was. They recorded her playing the drums and guitar and posted the clips on social media. The videos went viral! Even famous rock stars found out about her.

One of these rock stars, Lenny Kravitz, was so impressed he invited Nandi to jam with him in London one day. She could not contain her excitement! Lenny was one of her favorite musicians.

Nandi also got into an epic online rock battle with legendary drummer Dave Grohl, where they challenged each other to play songs.

In addition to jamming on the guitar and drums, she plays jazz and salsa and writes her own songs. "Nothing holds me back," says Nandi.

BORN APRIL 28, 2010
SOUTH AFRICA AND UNITED KINGDOM

"I LOVE TO WRITE MUSIC, AND MY BEATS ARE COLD!"
—NANDI BUSHELL

ILLUSTRATION BY
SHAREE MILLER

NAOMI OSAKA

TENNIS PLAYER

Once upon a time, there was a girl who could serve a tennis ball at more than 120 miles per hour—that's really, *really* fast. Naomi was born in Osaka, Japan, with wild, beautiful curly hair and brown skin. She was half-Haitian and half-Japanese, and people called her *hafu*—meaning "**mixed race**" or "half." But Naomi didn't feel half of anything. She felt like a whole person.

When she was a toddler, Naomi's family moved to Long Island, New York. Naomi and her older sister, Mari, watched tennis on television with their Haitian father, Leonard. The whole family admired tennis superstars Serena and Venus Williams, who were trained by their father. Soon Leonard began training Naomi and Mari to be top tennis players too. Naomi was just three years old.

When Naomi went pro, she proudly flew the Japanese flag. She didn't care that audiences were shocked when she, a brown-skinned girl, stepped up to play. She often played from the back of the court, using her sharp instincts and raw power to win set after set.

Naomi kept winning until she was face-to-face with her idol Serena Williams at the 2018 US Open. The match was electric to watch and grueling to play. And 20-year-old Naomi came out as the winner!

Tennis isn't the only thing that is important to Naomi. She cares deeply about **social justice** too. She has often refused to play matches to protest the unequal treatment of Black people in the United States.

Naomi is a fighter, and her biggest wins are yet to come.

BORN OCTOBER 16, 1997
JAPAN AND UNITED STATES OF AMERICA

"YOU JUST GOTTA KEEP GOING AND FIGHTING FOR EVERYTHING, AND ONE DAY YOU'LL GET TO WHERE YOU WANT."
—NAOMI OSAKA

ILLUSTRATION BY DANIELLE ELYSSE MANN

NIA FRANKLIN, KALIEGH GARRIS, CHESLIE KRYST, TONI-ANN SINGH, AND ZOZIBINI TUNZI

PAGEANT QUEENS

Once upon a time, five women changed the world's view of beauty. Meet Nia, Kaliegh, Cheslie, Toni-Ann, and Zozibini.

Nia loved singing and started writing music at just five years old! She wowed judges at her first pageant by singing her heart out. After many competitions, Nia won Miss America 2019.

Kaliegh was a shy child with curly hair who loved to dance. Years of straightening her curls damaged her hair, which led her to go natural. For the first time in 20 years, a Black girl with natural curly hair was crowned Miss Teen USA!

Cheslie was working as an attorney when she first competed for Miss North Carolina. She tried four times before winning. Then she took to the national stage as Miss USA.

Before vying for Miss World, Toni-Ann was busy taking women's studies classes. She is the fourth Jamaican woman to wear that crown.

As a little girl in South Africa, Zozibini never saw people who looked like her in magazines. But she wore her short hair with confidence and became the first woman with an Afro to win Miss Universe.

For the very first time in history, a Black woman won every major beauty pageant in the same year!

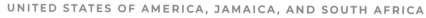

NIA FRANKLIN, BORN JULY 27, 1993; KALIEGH GARRIS, BORN AUGUST 21, 2000; CHESLIE KRYST, BORN APRIL 28, 1991; TONI-ANN SINGH, BORN FEBRUARY 1, 1996; ZOZIBINI TUNZI, BORN SEPTEMBER 18, 1993

UNITED STATES OF AMERICA, JAMAICA, AND SOUTH AFRICA

"BEAUTY IS NOT
JUST ONE THING."
—ZOZIBINI TUNZI

NZINGA OF NDONGO AND MATAMBA

QUEEN

Once upon a time, a girl was born to the ruling family of the Ndongo Kingdom in northern Angola. Her name was Nzinga. At the time, the kingdom had been taken over by the Portuguese, who kidnapped the locals and shipped them abroad for the slave trade.

Nzinga's father wanted her to be a strong, intelligent warrior. So Nzinga studied politics and Portuguese and learned how to fight.

After her father died, Nzinga's brother took over the throne but failed to defeat the Portuguese. He begged Nzinga to help him negotiate a peace treaty with them. Besides speaking Portuguese fluently, Nzinga was an excellent negotiator. She agreed.

When Nzinga arrived at the meeting, she saw the Portuguese governor sitting on a big chair. There was only a mat placed on the floor for her to sit on. Nzinga refused to let him make her feel inferior and did not sit on the floor. They agreed on a treaty, but it did not last long.

After her brother died, Nzinga became queen. She ruled for 40 years, fighting the Portuguese on and off the battlefield. She cleverly placed spies among the captured slaves. They would sneak information to her about the enemy army. She outsmarted her opponents again and again.

Queen Nzinga built a mighty kingdom and fought for her people well into old age. Angola later declared independence from Portuguese rule, and Angolans still celebrate Queen Nzinga as a fearless and heroic leader.

CIRCA 1583–DECEMBER 17, 1663
ANGOLA

ILLUSTRATION BY
JOELLE AVELINO

OCTAVIA E. BUTLER

AUTHOR

When Octavia was young, she saw a silly science fiction movie called *Devil Girl from Mars* and thought to herself, *I can write better than that.* So she did.

Octavia grew up in the fantastic world of comic books. She was a slow reader and an even slower writer. She had **dyslexia** and social anxiety, but she was determined to put her thoughts onto paper.

Despite her learning disability, Octavia earned a degree in history and studied creative writing at UCLA. She wrote chilling science fiction stories full of aliens, mutants, space journeys, vampires, and time travelers. Some of her characters had the power of telekinesis and could move things with their thoughts! None of her characters was perfect. They were flawed and messy, all fighting to survive. Octavia didn't believe in a simple world with happy endings.

Publishers didn't seem interested in work like this, especially from a Black woman who had trouble spelling. She received many rejections.

Octavia never stopped writing. Even if she had to work several jobs at a time, she got up in the wee hours of the morning to craft her stories. She wrote and rewrote each book, putting her characters in wild and dramatic situations.

In December 1975, she finally sold a book! She went on to publish 12 novels and nine short stories showcasing the wonders of her vivid imagination. The shy, dreamy kid from Pasadena, California, became a science fiction legend.

JUNE 22, 1947–FEBRUARY 24, 2006
UNITED STATES OF AMERICA

"EVERY STORY I CREATE CREATES ME. I WRITE TO CREATE MYSELF."
—OCTAVIA E. BUTLER

OCTAVIA E. BUTLER

ILLUSTRATION BY VALENCIA SPATES

OLIVE MORRIS

ACTIVIST

There once was a girl named Olive. She was born in Jamaica and moved to the Brixton neighborhood of London when she was nine years old. Many thought she was too outspoken, but really, she was brave. She stood up against injustice.

When she was 17, Olive saw an African man being harassed and beaten by the police. The law at the time allowed officers to stop people without any evidence that they'd done something wrong. The officers saw the color of the man's skin and assumed he'd stolen his expensive car. Horrified, Olive rushed over to help. The police handcuffed her, yet she still spoke out. So they arrested and beat her too.

Her work fighting **racism** was just beginning. She brought attention to **discrimination** in education, policing, and housing.

In 1972, many people in Brixton were on housing waiting lists. *Why?* thought Olive. Why were there homeless people or families living in awful conditions when there were plenty of vacant buildings? To raise awareness, Olive and other activists began squatting, or living in abandoned property. If they remained there long enough, they could claim rights to stay. That would be one way to get more people into the housing they needed!

While at Manchester University, Olive found other worthy causes. She worked with Black mothers to demand better education for their kids.

Although she died young, at age 27, Olive left behind an extraordinary **legacy**. "If she was alive," her sister said, "she would still be fighting."

JUNE 26, 1952–JULY 12, 1979
JAMAICA AND UNITED KINGDOM

"MY HEART WILL ALWAYS BE IN BRIXTON."
—OLIVE MORRIS

ILLUSTRATION BY
MONET KIFNER

PATRICIA BATH

OPHTHALMOLOGIST AND INVENTOR

Once there was a girl named Patricia who invented a device so the blind could see. It wasn't magic—it was science.

Her curiosity started with a chemistry set she got as a kid and was fueled by the hefty stack of books her mother gave her over the years.

Patricia sped through high school in two years and followed her path to medical school. Somewhere along the way, she became fascinated by eyesight and decided to specialize in **ophthalmology**. Working at a community clinic, she noticed that Black people were twice as likely to be blind or have poor vision as white people.

Why is that? Patricia wondered. She conducted a research study to find out. The answer was simple: lack of access to proper eye health care. She also found a solution. She trained volunteers to go out into the community to educate people on eye care and bring them to clinics. This simple solution saved a lot of people's sight.

Next, she set out to find a safer way to remove cataracts—a cloudy film that can grow over people's eyes and make their vision blurry. Left untreated, cataracts can cause blindness.

US doctors scoffed at her idea, so she headed to Europe. There, she perfected her device. Finally, in 1988, she patented the Laserphaco Probe. Her invention made eye surgery easier and less painful. With it, she could restore sight to people who had been blind for years.

Patricia wasn't held back by the doubts of others. She said, "Remember that the limits of science are not the limits of imagination."

 NOVEMBER 4, 1942–MAY 30, 2019
UNITED STATES OF AMERICA

"[MY PARENTS] BELIEVED THAT WITH ENOUGH EDUCATION, I COULD OWN THE WORLD."
—PATRICIA BATH

DR BATH

ILLUSTRATION BY
NAOMI ANDERSON-SUBRYAN

PHIONA MUTESI

CHESS PLAYER

Phiona was looking for food one day when she stumbled upon a sports club. To her surprise, she spotted her brother there playing a game of chess. The coach who ran the club, Robert, noticed Phiona peeking through the door and invited her in to play.

Phiona lived with her mother and two brothers in Katwe, a big slum in Uganda. Her mother couldn't afford school fees, so Phiona left school when she was six. She helped her mother sell maize to earn money for rice and tea and walked for two hours each day just to fetch clean water.

At first, Phiona played chess recklessly, sacrificing important pieces to win quickly. Coach Robert advised her to be more patient. Phiona listened, and within a year, she won matches against the top club player and against Coach Robert!

Phiona soon entered advanced competitions against university students and even national championships. At 11, she won her first championship and held the title for three years!

News about Phiona's skills spread fast. She and two teammates were invited to Africa's International Children's Chess Tournament in Sudan. They were the youngest team there and still took home the trophy.

A journalist wrote a book about Phiona that was adapted into a film called *Queen of Katwe*. With the money Phiona earned, she was able to buy her family a home and go back to school.

Phiona's coach taught her a skill that changed her life. Now Phiona teaches other kids how to play chess too.

BORN 1996

UGANDA

"WHEN I PLAY CHESS I'M NOT AFRAID. I KNOW THAT I CAN WIN."
—PHIONA MUTESI

ILLUSTRATION BY ONYINYE IWU

POLY STYRENE

PUNK ROCKER

Once there was a girl who rocked the underground punk music scene. Born to a Somalian father and a Scottish Irish mother, Marianne Joan Elliott-Said was naughty—and very creative—from the start. She used her sewing machine to make clothes from whatever she found at nearby thrift shops. She went out on adventures all on her own and starred in plays with her friends in the yard.

At 15, she dropped out of school and left home. She got into lots of trouble and got caught shoplifting. Instead of paying the fine, her mother insisted she complete community service. Her parents shipped her off to the country, and Mari ended up living off the land.

In 1977, she formed a band with people she met by putting out an ad for "Young Punx Who Want to Stick It Together." They named the band X-Ray Spex—a name right out of science fiction—and did things their own way. They paired the saxophones with whining guitar riffs. And Mari was one of only a few female lead vocalists in the punk music scene.

Punk music was fast, loud, and intense. Mari created a character for her stage image: Poly Styrene, named after a type of lightweight, disposable plastic. As Poly Styrene, she wore plastic dresses in vibrant orange, green, and pink. She covered her tight curls with an army helmet and sported clear plastic goggles. She had braces on her teeth and wore them with pride. She and her band played in smoky, grungy clubs and made posters out of newspaper clippings.

Poly finally found a place where she belonged.

JULY 3, 1957–APRIL 25, 2011
UNITED KINGDOM

ILLUSTRATION BY
KYLIE AKIA ERWIN

"I USED TO SING . . . TO STRAY
CATS. . . . THEY WERE MY FIRST
LIVE AUDIENCE."
—POLY STYRENE

QUEENDOM

PERFORMING ARTS GROUP

Little Asta grew up in Norway never seeing anyone who looked like her on television. With a Norwegian mother and a Ugandan father, she was treated differently because of her skin color. She often wondered where she fit in. But she wasn't alone.

In the mid 1990s, Asta joined an activist youth group fighting for **social justice**. There, she met other African Norwegian women. Some of the women were **biracial** with one Norwegian parent. Some had emigrated to Norway. All of them loved to write, act, and sing.

They each knew the pain of being made to feel like they didn't belong. But they refused to take it anymore. They were Black Norwegian women and members of the Norwegian community. They'd tell their own stories! In 1999, the friends formed the country's first all-female, all-Black performance group. They called it Queendom.

Using humor, live music, and poetry, they shared their struggles with **racism** and sexism. Over the years, Asta, Hannah, Monica, Haddy, and Isabell created four comedy theater productions, a TV show, a book, and an album. They also performed hundreds of concerts.

As time moved on, so did some of the original members. In 2019, the two remaining members of Queendom, Asta and Monica, released their album, *MamaLove*. They continue to perform the kid-friendly concert "Afropean Journey," with energetic songs that mix African styles with pop, soul, and reggae. "Stand up, queens!" they say. "The future will be shaped by microphones, pens, keyboards, and roaring voices."

FOUNDED IN 1999

NORWAY

"QUEENDOM IS A PLACE
WHERE THE QUEENS RULE!"
—QUEENDOM

ILLUSTRATION BY
NYANZA D

RITA BOSAHO

POLITICIAN

Baby Rita was born in a small country in central Africa called Equatorial Guinea. Home to gorillas, chimpanzees, leopards, crocodiles, and the biggest frogs on Earth, it is a tropical place. At the time, the country was ruled by Spain.

Rita was just four years old when her parents died. A Spanish military officer took her in, and she moved to Spain with her new **foster** family. Until university, she was always the only Black student in her class.

In Spain, Rita read many negative stories about Africans, but she never believed them. Her foster parents had taught her about equality and justice. She grew up and channeled her compassion for others into being a nurse.

When a political party in Spain said they wanted more people of color to join politics, Rita thought, *Why not give it a try?* She didn't have any political experience, but she knew this was an opportunity to push for justice for women and the less fortunate.

After 23 years of being a nurse, Rita added her name to the list of candidates for **parliament**. And she won, becoming the first Black woman in Spain's parliament!

"There are lots of people who don't understand that I'm Spanish. They see that I'm Black and think those two things can't go together," she said. Just by going to work every day, Rita's changing people's minds.

BORN MAY 21, 1965
EQUATORIAL GUINEA AND SPAIN

"WE ARE JUST ORDINARY PEOPLE WHO ARE TRYING TO CHANGE THIS COUNTRY'S INSTITUTIONS."
—RITA BOSAHO

ILLUSTRATION BY KEISHA MORRIS

ROSETTA THARPE

GUITARIST

Once there was a girl named Rosetta who was born to play the guitar. She plucked her first strings at age four. At six, she performed gospel music with her mother in churches around the South. Still tiny, she was lifted onto a piano so the audience could witness the "Guitar-Playing Miracle."

Rosetta first heard jazz and blues music after moving to Chicago. Wanting to play it all, she experimented and crafted a new sound. At the time, there weren't many female guitarists. And no one else was mixing religious and mainstream music like Rosetta.

Other singers performed gospel music only in church. Not Rosetta! She took her gospel songs to nightclubs and theaters. She charmed crowds, swinging her hips and making her electric guitar talk.

Known as Sister Rosetta Tharpe, she traveled the country and entertained packed audiences with her band. Because of **segregation**, she couldn't stay in the same hotels or eat at the same restaurants as her white bandmates. Regardless, Rosetta kept on rocking and had a rich, exciting 50-year-long career.

Though she was gospel's first superstar, Rosetta was also a rock and roll pioneer. Her music influenced other legendary rock stars. Elvis Presley studied her incredible picking. Chuck Berry imitated her style. And Johnny Cash declared she was one of his earliest heroes.

Sadly, Rosetta and her groundbreaking music were forgotten for a while. But now everyone knows she is the Godmother of Rock and Roll.

MARCH 20, 1915–OCTOBER 9, 1973
UNITED STATES OF AMERICA

ILLUSTRATION BY
AISHA AKEJU

"CAN'T NO MAN PLAY
LIKE ME. I PLAY BETTER
THAN A MAN."
—ROSETTA THARPE

ROXANNE SHANTÉ

Once upon a time, there was a girl who got into rhyming battles instead of fist fights.

In these rap battles, she said as many rhymes as she could think of as fast as she could. She used her words to slay the competition, win money, and make a name for herself around the neighborhood.

When she was 14, an influential DJ invited her to his studio to record her first single, "Roxanne's Revenge." She stepped up to the microphone and poured her feelings into her lyrics. On her first try, she made a song that sold more than 250,000 copies! After her breakout hit, she took the stage name Roxanne Shanté.

Her song started a rap battle, where rappers dissed each other back and forth. In the "Roxanne Wars," she usually came out on top.

People respected Roxanne for her ability to freestyle, or come up with rhymes on the spot. She won most of her rap battles, but many male rappers couldn't stand that she was better than them. One contest judge even gave her a low score just to keep her from winning.

Though Roxanne never got super rich, she earned respect. She made two solo albums and kept her skills sharp.

Sadly, she wasn't always paid what she was owed. But one day, she found a clause in an old contract that said her record company would pay for her education. She forced the company to honor the agreement and got her PhD in **psychology**. Roxanne paved the way for other female rappers and showed girls everywhere how to raise their voices with pride.

BORN NOVEMBER 9, 1969
UNITED STATES OF AMERICA

ILLUSTRATION BY
FANESHA FABRE

"I WOULD CALL MYSELF A
FEMINIST. . . . WE NEED TO
HEAR THAT. LITTLE GIRLS
NEED TO HEAR THAT."
—ROXANNE SHANTÉ

RUANE AND SHEILA JETER

INVENTORS

Ruane had a very special talent: she could turn an everyday object into something new. While learning how to design household products in college, she set her sights on the toaster.

She drew lots and lots of sketches, looking for the right design. Once the toaster was shaped like the letter V tilted onto its side, Ruane knew her idea was complete. She called it the Tiltster. The slots in the toaster now faced the user, making it easier to pop in bread, waffles, or bagels. There were no levers or knobs sticking out. Instead, it was the first toaster with a digital touch screen. That way, toast lovers could decide exactly how brown they wanted their bread to be.

Ruane knew she'd invented something brilliant, and she wanted to make sure no one could steal her design. To do that, she needed a patent. She filled out lots of paperwork and submitted detailed sketches. It took three years, but she got it!

This may have been Ruane's first invention, but it wasn't her last. She worked with others to design medical tools, like a type of scalpel for surgery. She also teamed up with her sister, Sheila, to improve designs for many home and office supplies. The sisters even created a handheld tool with multiple functions, made up of a stapler, staple remover, pencil sharpener, calculator, hole punch, tape measure, and scale!

These clever sisters may not be household names, but their ideas and designs are woven into the history of innovation.

RUANE JETER, BORN MAY 7, 1959
SHEILA JETER, BORN SEPTEMBER 5, 1955
UNITED STATES OF AMERICA

ILLUSTRATION BY
JONELL JOSHUA

"PRODUCT DEVELOPMENT:
IT'S MY PASSION."
—RUANE JETER

RUTH E. CARTER

COSTUME DESIGNER

With sketches, fabric, and sewing equipment, Ruth helped to create new worlds. She made costumes for historical figures, superheroes, and other movie characters. She dressed them in suits and shiny leather shoes, T-shirts and sneakers, sweeping African-patterned gowns, glittering beaded dresses, and—most famous of all—a sleek black uniform with cat ears and claws.

It all began when she was a kid. Ruth's mother sent her children to an after-school art program, where Ruth learned about African dances, drumming, poetry, and music. She started sketching out her own clothing designs, her fingers darkened by charcoal dust.

After college, she created costumes for theater productions and cared for the delicate fabrics. Once, she peeked out from backstage to see her mother standing there.

"You went four years to college to do laundry?" her mother asked.

"I'm still on my path, Mom," Ruth replied, trying not to roll her eyes.

Ruth's career wasn't anything like doing laundry. She read scripts carefully and took detailed notes. She searched archives for photographs and thoughtfully chose colors and patterns that fit the tone and time period of each film. For the movie *Black Panther*, she studied the fashion of African tribes—Xhosa, Zula, Himba, and Maasai.

Ruth has worked on more than 60 movies and television shows. She was nominated for an Oscar three times and finally won a shiny golden statue for her work on *Black Panther*.

BORN APRIL 10, 1960
UNITED STATES OF AMERICA

ILLUSTRATION BY
JEANETTA GONZALES

"I JUST WANT PEOPLE TO
LOOK AT MY FILMS FOR
NOW AND FOREVERMORE
AND KNOW THAT I WAS A
KEEPER OF THE CULTURE."
—RUTH E. CARTER

SAMARRIA BREVARD

SKATEBOARDER

Samarria's wild journey began on the basketball court of her apartment complex when she was 13 years old. She was shooting hoops when she spotted her brother and his friends doing skateboard tricks. She dropped her ball and called out, "Let me try!"

Right then, Samarria hopped on her first skateboard. It felt good to roll around on the asphalt. She liked it so much she bought herself a board and never looked back.

At first, she wasn't very good. She fell a lot and rolled and sprained her ankles. She couldn't do any tricks. It took hours and hours of practice to build up her skills.

Samarria started at skate parks and then moved to the streets of Southern California, where she found all sorts of exciting obstacles to conquer. She learned to launch herself into the air to soar over stairs or jump over a curb. Just like her video game heroes, she click-clacked over pavement and slid down steep railings. She picked up new skills from online videos and other skaters and became part of a tight-knit community focused on landing the gnarliest tricks possible.

Her favorite was the tre flip, an advanced move where the skateboarder kicks the board so it does an entire 360-degree spin while it flips before the skater lands back on it. Samarria mastered the move, and it helped her win a silver medal at the extreme sports competition called the X Games. Fans hope to see her land her breathtaking tricks at the Olympics some day.

BORN SEPTEMBER 22, 1993
UNITED STATES OF AMERICA

SANDRA AGUEBOR-EKPERUOH

MECHANIC

When Sandra was 13, she had an incredible dream. She woke up knowing that she was meant to fix cars.

Her parents told her to forget it. Girls weren't supposed to be mechanics, they said. Still, Sandra's father took her to his auto shop.

When they got there, she saw an engine that had been taken apart. It was covered in dark oil . . . and she immediately fell in love with it! She wanted to learn all about the engine and how to fix it. After that, Sandra worked at the auto shop every day after school.

Sandra's mother tried to keep her occupied with chores at home to tire her out, but Sandra was never too tired to work on a car. She'd do all her chores and then rush off to the repair shop.

Sandra grew up and opened her own garage.

She also started the Lady Mechanic Initiative to train other women in auto mechanics. After helping many women whose vehicles broke down in unsafe areas, Sandra wanted to make sure they'd never be stranded again. She mentors women from all backgrounds and ensures that they understand exactly how a car functions and how to fix it.

As the first female mechanic in Nigeria, Sandra has trained more than 700 women. These women are employed in garages across the country, showing the men working alongside them that, yes, of course it's possible for a woman to be a mechanic!

BORN 1972

NIGERIA

ILLUSTRATION BY
JONELL JOSHUA

"I AM LIKE A LOCOMOTIVE THAT
CANNOT BE STOPPED."
—ŞANDRA AGUEBOR-EKPERUOH

SANITÉ BÉLAIR

FREEDOM FIGHTER

In the 17th century, the French occupied an island called Saint-Domingue, now known as Haiti. They enslaved the locals, selling them to the highest bidder and forcing them to work on plantations. Tired of being mistreated, some of them ran into the mountains to hide, forming their own community. Known as the maroons, they helped free others by attacking French colonists and giving their fellow Haitians time to escape. A girl named Sanité was one of them.

At 15, Sanité married Charles Bélair, a brigade commander in the army of Toussaint Louverture, leader of the Haitian **revolution**. She and Charles fought side by side against the French for six years. A fierce fighter, she rose to the position of lieutenant in Toussaint's army.

The commander of the French militia set out to crush the Haitian resistance. He wanted the enslaved population to know that if they dared to seek freedom, they would die!

Sanité and her fellow maroons did not back down.

When Sanité was captured, Charles gave himself up so they wouldn't be separated. The pair was tried in front of an audience. Charles was sentenced to death by firing squad, and Sanité was to be beheaded.

Sanité refused to put her head on the chopping block. She insisted that she had a right to an honorable soldier's death by firing squad, just like her husband. She also refused to wear a blindfold as she was led to her death. As the soldiers prepared to fire, Sanité yelled out, "Long live freedom! Down with slavery!"

CIRCA 1781–OCTOBER 5, 1802

HAITI

ILLUSTRATION BY
ANJINI MAXWELL

"LONG LIVE
FREEDOM! DOWN
WITH SLAVERY!"
—SANITÉ BÉLAIR

SASHA HUBER

ARTIST

Sasha's family was a rich tapestry. She had relatives from 10 countries! She grew up in Switzerland, where her father was from, but always felt connected to her mother's home country, Haiti.

Girls at Sasha's school typically took crafts classes, but she opted to join the boys' technical drawing class instead. A talented student, she decided to make art her career. She studied graphic design in university and worked as a visual artist in Switzerland, Italy, and Finland.

Sasha based a lot of her work on Haiti's **colonial** history. She used a staple gun to make portraits of Christopher Columbus and the British rulers who took over Haiti a long time ago. To her, the staple gun was like a weapon. It reminded her of the pain of the enslaved Haitians.

One day, Sasha's sister gave her a book about the slave trade in Switzerland, a topic that was never taught to her in school. She read that the Agassizhorn mountain peak in Switzerland was named after glaciologist Louis Agassiz. He had been a respected scientist. He was also a terrible racist, known for mistreating and humiliating enslaved people in the 19th century. Sasha joined the book's author in a campaign to rename the peak after Renty, a man enslaved by Louis.

Sasha engraved Renty's story on a metal plaque, got in a helicopter, and flew to the mountain peak. She waded through the thick snow to the spot where a plaque with Louis's name stood. She removed the old plaque and put the new one in its place.

Sasha believes that making great art can make great change.

BORN APRIL 24, 1975

SWITZERLAND AND FINLAND

ILLUSTRATION BY
TIFFANY BAKER

"YOU CAN CREATE A
WORLD EXACTLY HOW YOU
WANT IT TO BE, AND THIS
MAKES IT REAL."
—SASHA HUBER

SHIRLEY CHISHOLM

POLITICIAN

Shirley was born to **immigrant** parents in New York City. But as a child, she also got to spend seven wonderful years on the lush island of Barbados with her grandmother. There, she gained a new accent, a strong education, and boundless confidence.

In college, Shirley was frustrated that women were never elected to student council. So she campaigned for two women when they ran for office. She also helped create a social group for Black women, because they weren't allowed in clubs with white students.

After graduation, Shirley worked in education and gave her time and energy to many community activist and political groups. After 20 years, she decided to run for office. Her star was on the rise! In 1964, Shirley joined the New York State Assembly. Four years later, she became the first Black woman elected to the US Congress!

In 1972, Shirley changed the world again—as the first woman and the first Black person to run for US president as part of a major party. With fiery determination, she launched her "Unbought and Unbossed" campaign. Her slogan made it clear that she answered only to the American people. She didn't have much money, and she had to deal with angry threats and gender **discrimination**, but she never gave up. She even sued—and won—to participate in a televised debate!

Although she lost the Democratic nomination, Shirley remained in Congress for seven terms, where she boldly advocated for those often ignored: women, minorities, and the poor.

NOVEMBER 30, 1924–JANUARY 1, 2005
UNITED STATES OF AMERICA

ILLUSTRATION BY
OLIVIA FIELDS

"IF THEY DON'T GIVE YOU
A SEAT AT THE TABLE,
BRING A FOLDING CHAIR."
—SHIRLEY CHISHOLM

SIMONE MANUEL

SWIMMER

At four years old, Simone stood at the edge of the pool looking at all the other families. The shimmering water at her feet looked dangerous and enchanting.

Once Simone got in the pool, she loved it. She swam clear across the pool on her second day of lessons. She tried out ballet, volleyball, soccer, basketball—but always came back to the water.

By nine, Simone joined a local swim team and started competing. Her muscled arms cut through the water in graceful swoops. The more she trained, the faster she became. But she looked around and wondered, *Why don't any of the other swimmers look like me?*

She kept swimming, and soon she was ready for national and international competitions. She even made it into the record books a few times before graduating from high school. Still, Simone felt out of place in swimming. It was uncomfortable being known as "the Black swimmer." Why couldn't she just be Simone the swimmer?

Simone joined her university team. Then, at 19 years old, she qualified for the 2016 Olympics. In the 100-meter race, Simone flew across the pool in 52 seconds. She touched the wall at the very same moment as another swimmer. Together, they broke a record and tied for gold!

The first Black woman to win an Olympic gold medal in swimming, Simone said, "This medal is not just for me. It's for all the people who came before me . . . and it's for all the people who come after me who believe they can't do it."

BORN AUGUST 2, 1996
UNITED STATES OF AMERICA

"LET YOUR PASSION
BE YOUR COMPASS
TO ACHIEVING THE
IMPOSSIBLE."
—SIMONE MANUEL

ILLUSTRATION BY
DANIELLE ELYSSE MANN

SONIA GUIMARÃES

PHYSICS PROFESSOR

Once upon a time, there was a girl called Sonia who looked for the answers to any problem she saw.

Sonia was great at math and thought she wanted to be an engineer. She was the first person in her family to go to college, and there she found a new love: **physics**. So she switched course and found herself as one of only five women in a physics class with 50 men.

She had no problem mastering the work, but she found that other people made assumptions about her based on her skin color and her gender. A teacher once told her that women did not need physics in life so she should not bother trying to get a scholarship. Sonia applied for the scholarship anyway.

When Sonia graduated from her PhD program in England, she became the first Black Brazilian doctor of physics. She returned to Brazil and joined the country's main technological institute as their first Black professor. At the time, the school did not even accept female students.

Many members of the faculty were cruel to Sonia. They complained about the way she dressed and called her a bad teacher. No one came to her defense. She was transferred to another school. Later, when the person responsible for her transfer retired, Sonia returned to the institute and got his job!

Sonia has published her groundbreaking research in international scientific journals. She supports other women who work in the sciences. And she still searches for solutions to any problem she sees.

BORN JUNE 20, 1956
BRAZIL

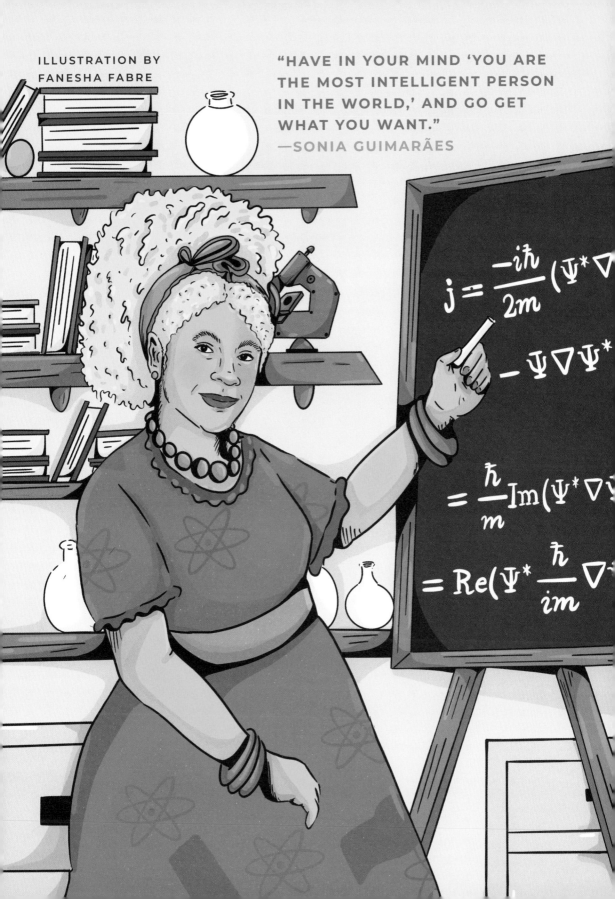

ILLUSTRATION BY
FANESHA FABRE

"HAVE IN YOUR MIND 'YOU ARE
THE MOST INTELLIGENT PERSON
IN THE WORLD,' AND GO GET
WHAT YOU WANT."
—SONIA GUIMARÃES

$$j = \frac{-i\hbar}{2m}(\Psi^* \nabla$$

$$- \Psi \nabla \Psi^*$$

$$= \frac{\hbar}{m} \text{Im}(\Psi^* \nabla \Psi$$

$$= \text{Re}(\Psi^* \frac{\hbar}{im} \nabla$$

STEFFI JONES

SOCCER PLAYER

All Steffi ever wanted to do was play soccer. The daughter of a German mother and a Black American soldier, she and her brothers were raised by their mother. They lived in a poor area in Germany.

She started playing soccer with her older brother when she was just four years old. Her mother believed soccer was a "boys' sport," but Steffi kept at it. In school, she was teased because of the color of her skin. Playing soccer helped her gain the confidence to stand up for herself and others. Her grades also improved. Her mother noticed these changes and started supporting her daughter's love for soccer.

Steffi didn't even know there were soccer teams for girls until she was 14. And in 1993, she joined Germany's national women's team. She played in 111 international matches and won two Olympic bronze medals. But even as a world champion, she still faced **racism**. Once after a game, she high-fived a fan who then called her names. Shocked, she didn't respond. Her teammates rushed over and stood up for her. She said that knowing the team was behind her was a great feeling.

After 31 years, Steffi stopped playing soccer. She became the first Afro-German to coach the women's national soccer team.

On and off the field, Steffi has fought for racial integration and tolerance. She has visited schools and spoken about equality and her experiences. One of the best defenders in soccer, Steffi is also a defender of the rights of women and Afro-Germans.

BORN DECEMBER 22, 1972

GERMANY

"SOCCER IS A SPORT THAT ENABLES GIRLS AND WOMEN TO BUILD THEIR STRENGTH AND TO DEVELOP IMPORTANT LIFE SKILLS."
—STEFFI JONES

ILLUSTRATION BY LINDSEY BAILEY

SUAD ALI

POLITICAL SCIENTIST AND AUTHOR

Once there was a girl named Suad who traveled halfway across the world but never forgot where she came from. Suad was born in Somalia during a terrible civil war. When she was three years old, her father made the difficult decision to flee their homeland. He put his family on a plane, and they all traveled to Sweden.

In grade school, Suad wanted to be student council president, but her teacher told her not to even try. The teacher said she did not speak Swedish well because she was a foreigner. Suad was confused. She'd been in Sweden for nearly her entire life! She could read and write the language perfectly.

At her university, people advised her to study science. They said it would guarantee her a good career. But Suad knew exactly what she wanted to do. She wanted to work with the United Nations (UN) and fight for equality and human rights. She already spoke multiple languages and understood more than one culture, but she didn't know if they'd ever hire a Black girl wearing a **hijab**.

In 2011, a terrible famine hit Somalia. It left many people hungry and sick. Suad knew she had to help. She knocked on every door in her neighborhood, asking for donations. And she raised $6,000! Suad gave the money to the Red Cross so it could buy supplies and food to help the Somali people.

Eventually, Suad joined the UN, doing her best to provide aid to anyone in need. She also wrote a novel about the **refugee** experience.

BORN OCTOBER 5, 1990

SOMALIA AND SWEDEN

"NO ONE IS YOU, AND THAT'S YOUR POWER."
—SUAD ALI

ILLUSTRATION BY
ANJINI MAXWELL

SUSANA BACA

SINGER

Once upon a time in South America, enslaved Peruvians were forced to abandon their culture. After slavery ended, Afro-Peruvians were often treated like second-class citizens. Many were not proud of being Black. A girl named Susana wanted to change that.

Susana grew up in a poor Afro-Peruvian community. Her father played the guitar, and her mother loved to dance. Susana watched and learned from them. Performing for neighbors, she'd sing into a microphone made from a can placed on the end of a stick.

Her mother discouraged her from becoming a singer, so Susana became a teacher. But over time, she found herself singing more and more. Instead of pop music, Susana sang traditional Afro-Peruvian songs. She mixed historical folk music with modern rhythms and often used poetry as lyrics. When she couldn't get a recording contract, Susana and her husband recorded one of her concerts and created their own record label to release her songs.

Everything changed when a famous American musician put together a collection of Afro-Peruvian songs. It included Susana's version of "Maria Lando," which became an international hit!

Susana tours the world, delighting audiences with her soulful voice. She glides barefoot across the stage in flowing gowns. Her somber lyrics about Black pride are backed by the rhythm of the *cajón*, a box-shaped drum that a musician sits on and beats with their hands.

She shares the music of her ancestors with dignity and joy.

BORN MAY 24, 1944
PERU

"I EXPRESS MYSELF WITH THE SONGS AND POETRY OF MY PEOPLE."
—SUSANA BACA

ILLUSTRATION BY NOKWANDA THEMBA

TANIA J. LEÓN FERRÁN

COMPOSER AND CONDUCTOR

Once upon a time, a girl received a gift that changed her life. Tania's grandmother knew she had a special musical talent. She convinced the local conservatory to begin training Tania when she was just four years old. A year later, her grandfather gave her a piano. Tania's legs were so short they could barely reach the pedals!

She studied hard and became a marvelous classical pianist. Her musical skills even earned her a full scholarship to a university in the United States.

Tania thought she'd found her career in playing classical music, but her path changed when Arthur Mitchell, the first Black principal dancer at the New York City Ballet, insisted she write music for his new show. She took on the challenge—and liked it so much that she began composing her own pieces. The music, words, and stories flowed from Tania's fingertips almost faster than she could scribble them down.

Then Arthur asked her if she'd like to lead the orchestra for a performance in Italy. Tania accepted. She waved the conducting baton as if she were weaving a magic spell over the audience. She commanded the orchestra pit like a queen. The next day her face was splashed across Italian newspapers with a new title: conductor.

Tania's music tells stories of moments in history. She travels the world, sharing sounds from her Cuban, Spanish, Chinese, and African ancestors, firm in the belief that music can break down borders between people and unite them as members of the human race.

BORN MAY 14, 1943
CUBA AND UNITED STATES OF AMERICA

"THERE IS ACTUALLY ANOTHER LEVEL BY WHICH WE COMMUNICATE, MUSICIAN TO MUSICIAN, AND WHEN WE REACH IT, IT'S JUST SPECTACULAR."
—TANIA J. LEÓN FERRÁN

ILLUSTRATION BY KEISHA MORRIS

TAYTU BETUL

EMPRESS

Taytu was born in Ethiopia, a country filled with tree-covered highlands, enormous lakes, bustling savannas, beautiful deserts, and fiery volcanoes. Her family was related to the **dynasty** that ruled the Ethiopian empire.

An intelligent woman, Taytu could read and write in Amharic, her country's native language—a rare skill among women at the time. Taytu loved her country and its vibrant culture. She married Menelik II, who became the emperor of Ethiopia.

Menelik and his trusted adviser Taytu watched as European countries took over African nations all over the continent. To protect Ethiopia, Menelik decided to sign a treaty with Italy. The two countries would be allies and trade partners. Taytu was skeptical.

The pair soon discovered that the treaty was a trick! The Amharic version of the treaty recognized Ethiopia as an independent country, but the Italian version said that Italy had control over the nation.

Taytu was furious! She tore the treaty to pieces.

A few years later, the nations prepared to fight. Advisors said Taytu should stay at home and keep people calm. She ignored them and rode her horse to the front lines of the Battle of Adwa. She commanded thousands of soldiers and mobilized others to care for the wounded.

Praised as "the Light of Ethiopia," Empress Taytu changed the course of history. Her strength and strategy helped her side win the battle!

Ethiopia is the only country in Africa that was never colonized.

CIRCA 1851–FEBRUARY 11, 1918
ETHIOPIA

· 198 ·

ILLUSTRATION BY
GABRIELLE TESFAYE

THOKOZILE MUWAMBA

FIGHTER PILOT

Once upon a time, there was a little girl who wanted to see the world from a bird's-eye view. Thokozile yearned to fly the big jets she would see in the sky. It was an ambitious dream for a young girl living in Zambia, but she didn't waver from her goal.

After high school, Thokozile could not afford to go straight into flight training, so she enrolled at a local university to study math and science.

In her first year of school, Thokozile heard that the Zambian Air Force was recruiting women to train as fighter pilots. This was her chance! Thokozile did not waste any time sending in her application, and she was chosen to join!

Thokozile had an aunt who was a pilot. Her aunt mentored her and gave her tips on staying calm while flying. After standard military training, Thokozile spent two years in flight training. It was tough, but she loved doing things that challenged her.

During her very first flight, Thokozile was nervous and scared, but she remembered her aunt's wise words, took a deep breath, and flew the plane confidently. Her first flight was a success! She smiled ear to ear as she landed the plane with ease.

A few years after her training, Thokozile became an official fighter pilot—the first female fighter pilot in Zambia! An inspiration to all women and girls who dream of soaring through the skies, Thokozile is ready for her next challenge: becoming Zambia's first female air force commander.

BORN MARCH 6, 1992
ZAMBIA

"I HOPE TO INSPIRE MORE WOMEN TO TAKE UP CHALLENGING ROLES IN SOCIETY."
—THOKOZILE MUWUMBA

ILLUSTRATION BY ASHLEIGH CORRIN

TONI MORRISON

AUTHOR

When Toni was in high school, she always had her nose in a book. She worked at the library, shelving books. Instead of getting in trouble for reading all the time, she got a promotion.

At Howard University, she acted in Shakespeare plays and read great literature. There was just one problem. Her professors didn't teach anything by Black writers.

Toni taught literature for a while, but then she saw an ad for a position that seemed perfect: book editor. Editors decide which stories get published. Toni thought it was time to see the words of Black writers in bookstores everywhere. While she published works by famous thinkers and activists, she stayed out of the spotlight to let her authors shine.

Each and every day, Toni wrote. She jotted down notes while sitting in traffic, at meetings, and at the dinner table. Even though she worked at a publishing company, she secretly released her first novel, *The Bluest Eye*, in 1970 with a different company. Her colleagues immediately recognized her talent and asked to publish the rest of her work.

Toni wrote 11 novels, several children's books, and a few collections of short stories. All of them were works of art about Black struggles, joyful lives, and the emotional scars of **racism**.

In 1993, a friend called to tell Toni she'd won the Nobel Prize in Literature for her many poetic and moving novels. Toni didn't believe it and hung up. But it was true! Today her books are the ones shelved in homes, bookstores, and libraries all over the world.

FEBRUARY 18, 1931–AUGUST 5, 2019
UNITED STATES OF AMERICA

ILLUSTRATION BY
NOA DENMON

"IF YOU FIND A BOOK YOU
REALLY WANT TO READ
BUT IT HASN'T BEEN
WRITTEN YET, THEN YOU
MUST WRITE IT."
—TONI MORRISON

THE VILLAGE OF UMOJA

ALL-WOMEN COMMUNITY

Once upon a time, a group of women banded together to create a place that would be safe for women and girls. It all began when a girl named Rebecca got married very young. The Samburu community, where she was from, had a tradition of arranging marriages between young girls and older men.

Rebecca didn't like how women were treated in the village. She often showed other women how to stand up for themselves. Angry, the men came together to punish her. Her husband didn't even defend her as she was beaten. So she left him and formed her own village—one where women would work together and protect one another.

That village is called Umoja, which means "unity" in Swahili. Other women who'd been mistreated joined the all-women village. In Samburu culture, women have no rights. They are treated like property and not as human beings. But in Umoja, they're given the respect and support they deserve.

The women of Umoja build their own homes and raise their children together. While the children play outside, the adults pass the time singing and dancing to traditional songs.

To earn money, the villagers design exquisite beaded jewelry that they sell to tourists. The money is shared among them, and anything extra is kept for emergencies. They built a school with their earnings, and children from Umoja and nearby areas get free education there.

Umoja is the only all-women village in the world.

FORMED IN 1990

KENYA

"WE HAVE TO BE PROUD THAT WE ARE WOMEN."
—REBECCA LOLOSOLI

ILLUSTRATION BY
BRIA NICOLE

VIOLA DAVIS

ACTOR

Once there was a girl named Viola who grew up extremely poor. She often went hungry and unwashed. Hers was the only Black family in town. Bullied and called horrible names, she felt worthless. But she found a way to escape.

Viola gazed in awe when she saw Cicely Tyson in a movie. It was the first time she'd seen an actor who looked like her, with dark skin and full lips. She immediately wanted to act. At eight years old, Viola entered a local skit contest with her sisters and won!

After studying theater in college, she landed her first role in a Broadway show. She was so stressed out about her performance, though, that half of her hair fell out. Her acting, however, was magnificent. She was even nominated for an award!

Viola's film and television career took more effort, but she kept at it. Her dreams were bigger than her fear.

Over time, she played a nurse, a lawyer, a legendary blues singer, and more. No matter the role, Viola always gave 100 percent. When she played a mother facing tough choices in a seven-and-a-half-minute scene, she prepared by writing a 50-page character biography!

Critics and audiences love her. She's the only Black woman to have won the top awards for acting in a movie, TV show, and Broadway play.

Viola blazed her own path out of poverty to build a successful career. Like Cicely Tyson was for her, she's a shining star for all little girls fighting to be seen.

BORN AUGUST 11, 1965
UNITED STATES OF AMERICA

ILLUSTRATION BY JOHNALYNN HOLLAND

"I SEE MYSELF IN SO MANY KIDS WHO WANT TO GO OUT AND BE SOMEBODY."
—VIOLA DAVIS

VIOLA DESMOND

ENTREPRENEUR AND ACTIVIST

Growing up in Nova Scotia, a province in eastern Canada, Viola noticed that ads for hair products showed only white people. She wanted to open a salon for Black women. But because she was Black, Viola could not find a local beauty school that would admit her. So she traveled to Montreal, Atlantic City, and New York City to take courses. She even trained with the legendary Madam C. J. Walker!

Later, Viola returned home and opened the city's first Black hair salon for women. But she wanted to do more. So she opened up a school to teach Black women business skills and help them find employment.

One night, Viola went to the movies. She asked to sit near the screen because it was easier for her to see. But the ticket seller would not sell her a ticket on the main floor. So she bought the balcony ticket he offered her and took a seat in the front of the theater anyway. The manager told her she had to move. The front section, he explained, was for white people only. He said if she didn't move, he would call the police.

Viola refused to move.

Once the police arrived, they grabbed her, dragged her out, and threw her in jail for the night. She was fined for not paying the correct amount of tax for the downstairs ticket (though she had offered to). She tried to sue the theater for **discrimination** but did not get justice.

Viola's courage was not forgotten. Decades later, the Canadian government pardoned her, and in 2018, it honored Viola for her defiance of **racism** and her fight for justice by putting her picture on the $10 bill.

JULY 6, 1914–FEBRUARY 7, 1965

CANADA

WARSAN SHIRE

POET

Once upon a time, there was a Somali girl named Warsan who was born in Kenya. Her parents had been forced to leave Somalia because war broke out in the country. Together, her family immigrated to London as **refugees**.

Warsan felt like an outsider growing up in London. It made her think about the true meaning of "home."

She fell in love with writing and decided to channel her thoughts into poetry. "When I was younger," Warsan said, "I wanted to read something somewhere that I could see myself in." But she couldn't find the stories she wanted, so she decided to write them herself! She'd use her own storytelling skills to tell the tales of families like hers. She wanted the world to know that refugees go on dangerous journeys to new countries only when they no longer feel safe or have no other choice.

Her poetry highlights people in her family and community—like the woman in a **hijab** she saw on a bus pushing a baby carriage or her family members who fought through war and conflict to establish new homes away from home. To capture the stories her relatives share, Warsan carries a small cassette recorder called a Dictaphone. Listening closely to their words, laughs, and groans, she turns their pain and their triumphs into insightful poems.

Warsan is the first Young Poet Laureate for London. She has published books of poetry and performed all around the world. Her words were even included in an album by the superstar singer Beyoncé.

BORN AUGUST 1, 1988
SOMALIA AND UNITED KINGDOM

"DON'T ASSUME, ASK. BE KIND. TELL THE TRUTH. DON'T SAY ANYTHING YOU CAN'T STAND BEHIND FULLY. HAVE INTEGRITY. TELL PEOPLE HOW YOU FEEL."
—WARSAN SHIRE

ILLUSTRATION BY
CAMILLA RU

YETNEBERSH NIGUSSIE

LAWYER

When Yetnebersh was just five years old, her life changed dramatically. She got a terrible infection that left her blind. But she went to a special school, where she played and laughed, learned and grew, just like any other child.

A smart student, Yetnebersh grew to be a leader. In high school, she ran the student council. And in college, at Addis Ababa University, she launched the school's first female student's association—and became its president. Yetnebersh noticed how women and people with disabilities were treated disrespectfully, and she wanted to do everything in her power to change that. "I started my fight, not by telling people, but by showing people that I'm able to contribute," she said. "I have one disability, but I have 99 abilities."

She earned her law degree and master's degree in social work and, after volunteering with dozens of disability groups, Yetnebersh cofounded an organization to provide help and services to people with disabilities. It also pushed companies, the Ethiopian government, and society at large to understand their needs.

To provide more support for students, she opened a school for underprivileged children in the country's capital, Addis Ababa.

Organizations all over the world have called on Yetnebersh to help them do better. However, her main focus remains on Ethiopia. She wants young people throughout the country to follow her lead and use their many varied abilities to improve their own communities.

BORN JANUARY 24, 1982
ETHIOPIA

"SCHOOLS ARE THE RIGHT PLACE TO PROMOTE INCLUSION OF PERSONS WITH DISABILITIES."
—YETNEBERSH NIGUSSIE

ILLUSTRATION BY TIFFANY BAKER

ZAHRA BANI

JAVELIN THROWER

There once was a girl named Zahra who was born in Somalia. Her name meant "flower" in Arabic. When she was 10 years old, she moved to Italy with her family. There, she trained and trained and blossomed into a fierce competitor in the javelin throw.

When athletes compete in this track and field event, they launch a light metal-tipped spear—or javelin—as far as they can. Long ago, the javelin was used to hunt. Eventually, throwing the spear became a sport featured in the Olympic Games as far back as 708 BCE. Because the athlete runs before releasing the spear, the javelin can reach speeds close to 70 miles per hour. A single throw can cover a distance longer than a football field!

On a cloudy day at the 2005 World Championships, Zahra took several deep breaths before her final throw. She gripped the javelin in one hand over her shoulder and took off. As she neared the foul line, she threw the seven-foot-long spear as hard as she could. Zahra yelled as the javelin soared through the air. She didn't win a medal, but she still smiled big. She'd achieved her personal best throw of 62.75 meters.

Zahra won her event at the Italian Athletics Championships seven times. She also received a medal for being the best at javelin.

Proud and motivated, Zahra posted on social media: "Even on Sundays you train." Yet she still made time to have fun with friends, dressing up for birthday dinners and going to see Beyoncé in concert!

In both work and play, Zahra inspires girls to live their best lives.

BORN DECEMBER 31, 1979
SOMALIA AND ITALY

"I'M PROUD TO BE AN
EXAMPLE FOR YOUNG
PEOPLE. MY ENTHUSIASM
WILL NEVER STOP."
—ZAHRA BANI

MEET MORE REBELS!

The first volume of Good Night Stories for Rebel Girls features 100 tales of extraordinary women, including these barrier-breaking Black women.

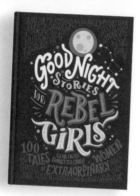

ALEK WEK

Once upon a time, a girl named Alek escaped war in South Sudan. As a supermodel, her dark skin made her an instant sensation.

Illustration by Bijou Karman

BALKISSA CHAIBOU

Once there was a girl called Balkissa who wanted to become a doctor. She fought hard against her arranged marriage to attend school.

Illustration by Priya Kuriyan

FADUMO DAYIB

Fadumo's childhood was spent trying to escape from war. She grew up to become Somalia's first female presidential candidate.

Illustration by Lea Heinrich

HARRIET TUBMAN

Once there was a girl who escaped from slavery. Over the course of 11 years, Harriet rescued hundreds of enslaved people.

Illustration by Sally Nixon

HATSHEPSUT

The powerful Hatshepsut was the first woman to ever become pharaoh. She ruled Egypt for 25 years.

Illustration by Eleni Kalorkoti

MAE C. JEMISON

Once there was a curious girl named Mae who trained to be a doctor and an astronaut. She was the first Black woman in space.

Illustration by Alexandra Bowman

MAYA ANGELOU

There was a girl named Maya who didn't speak for five years. She became a renowned writer and a major voice in the US civil rights movement.

Illustration by Thandiwe Tshabalala

MELBA LISTON

Once there was a girl named Melba who loved jazz. She wowed audiences as the first female trombonist to play in big bands.

Illustration by Alice Barberini

MICHAELA DEPRINCE

Michaela was mistreated because of her skin condition. She chased her dream of being a ballerina and joined the Dutch National Ballet.

Illustration by Debora Guidi

MICHELLE OBAMA

Once there was a girl named Michelle who aimed high. She inspired countless girls as the first Black First Lady of the United States.

Illustration by Marta Signori

MIRIAM MAKEBA

Miriam used her music to bring attention to the suffering caused by apartheid. People called her "Mama Africa."

Illustration by Helena Morais Soares

MISTY COPELAND

A young girl named Misty loved dancing. Even after an injury, she became the first Black principal dancer at the American Ballet Theatre.

Illustration by Ping Zhu

NANNY OF THE MAROONS

Queen Nanny led a group of escaped slaves called the maroons. Together, they built a village called Nanny Town.

Illustration by Jeanetta Gonzales

NINA SIMONE

Nina wanted Black people to be proud and free. An acclaimed jazz singer, she poured her passion into music.

Illustration by T.S. Abe

ROSA PARKS

Rosa refused to give up her seat on the bus. This act incited a boycott that led to the end of bus segregation.

Illustration by Sally Nixon

SERENA & VENUS WILLIAMS

Once there were sisters named Serena and Venus who loved playing tennis. They won enough games to each be ranked #1 in the world!

Illustration by Debora Guidi

SIMONE BILES

Once there was a girl who flew through the air. Her name was Simone, and she was the greatest gymnast in US history.

Illustration by Eline Van Dam

WANGARI MAATHAI

Wangari planted trees to save her Kenyan village. Her act ignited a widespread movement across Africa.

Illustration by Thandiwe Tshabalala

WILMA RUDOLPH

Once a girl named Wilma had a paralyzed leg. She did not let that stop her from becoming the fastest woman in the world.

Illustration by Alice Barberini

YAA ASANTEWAA

In a land of gold, a queen named Yaa led an army of 5,000. People still sing about her fighting spirit today.

Illustration by Noa Snir

Fans helped us choose the subjects to feature in *Good Night Stories for Rebel Girls Volume 2*, including these phenomenal women.

ALICE BALL

Once upon a time, a chemist named Alice found a cure for a terrible disease. Her amazing contribution was finally recognized many years later.

Illustration by Martina Paukova

BEYONCÉ

Once there was a girl named Beyoncé who sang for audiences in her home. As the most influential living pop star in the world, she delights fans with her music, videos, and performances.

Illustration by Eline Van Dam

BLACK MAMBAS

The Black Mambas were rangers who stopped poachers in the South African savanna. These heroes kept wild animals safe.

Illustration by Alice Beniero

CELIA CRUZ

Once upon a time, a girl named Celia sang her siblings to sleep. She eventually became the Queen of Salsa.

Illustration by Ping Zhu

CHIMAMANDA NGOZI ADICHIE

A girl named Chimamanda wrote stories about Nigeria, migration, gender, and war. People shared her words with one another to feel empowered.

Illustration by T.S. Abe

CLEMANTINE WAMARIYA

Once a girl named Clemantine listened to the magical stories her grandmother told her. She grew up to become a storyteller and activist, helping refugees.

Illustration by Alice Barberini

KATHERINE JOHNSON, DOROTHY VAUGHAN, MARY JACKSON

Computer scientists Katherine, Dorothy, and Mary helped launch an astronaut into space. They are three of the most inspiring figures in space travel.

Illustration by Cristina Portolano

KHOUDIA DIOP

Once upon a time, a girl called Khoudia was teased because of her dark skin. She became a model and campaigned to prevent bullying.

Illustration by Debora Guidi

LEYMAH GBOWEE

Leymah was a single mother who led a group of women for peace. Together, they stopped a war.

Illustration by Thandiwe Tshabalala

MADAM C. J. WALKER

Once there was a girl who wanted to keep Black hair healthy. She called herself Madam C.J. Walker and built a hugely successful business.

Illustration by Cristina Spanò

MARY FIELDS

Once there was a girl who always helped others. She became a fearless mail carrier with the nickname "Stagecoach Mary."

Illustration by Amari Mitnaul

MARY SEACOLE

A girl named Mary loved to "cure" her dolls. As a nurse at the front lines during the Crimean War, she saved many lives.

Illustration by Annalisa Ventura

NEFERTITI

Nefertiti was a mysterious queen who reigned Egypt until she disappeared. Some believe she disguised herself as a man.

Illustration by Eleni Kalorkoti

OPRAH WINFREY

Once there was a little girl with a big voice. Oprah became the queen of talk shows and a generous philanthropist.

Illustration by T.S. Abe

RUBY NELL BRIDGES

Once upon a time, a girl called Ruby wanted to learn. She faced down bullies as the first Black student to desegregate an all-white elementary school.

Illustration by Giulia Tomai

SOJOURNER TRUTH

Sojourner traveled across the United States to give speeches on equal rights. In her most famous speech, she asked, "Ain't I a woman?"

Illustration by Cristina Amodeo

VALERIE THOMAS

There once was a girl named Valerie who loved space. She came up with a brilliant invention called the illusion transmitter.

Illustration by Fanesha Fabre

Good Night Stories for Rebel Girls: 100 Immigrant Women Who Changed the World tells the stories of remarkable women who left their home countries and made their mark, including these women who dared to follow their dreams.

ANNE WAFULA STRIKE

Once there was a girl called Anne who became sick and paralyzed. She refused to stop moving and won a medal at the Paralympic World Cup.

Illustration by Luisa Rivera

CHINWE ESIMAI

A girl named Chinwe noticed immigrants like her often tried blending into the crowd. She started a blog to help immigrant women become leaders.

Illustration by D'Ara Nazaryan

CLAUDIA RANKINE

Claudia addresses difficult topics in her writing. She's won many awards for her poetry.

Illustration by Nicole Miles

EDMONIA LEWIS

Once upon a time, there was a girl of African and Native American descent. Edmonia was the first woman of color in the US to be a professional sculptor.

Illustration by Monica Ahanonu

ELIZABETH NYAMAYARO

When she was a girl, Elizabeth dreamed of working for the United Nations. Her wish came true! She worked on a worldwide campaign for gender equity.

Illustration by Marian Bailey

HAZEL SCOTT

There once was a girl named Hazel who could play piano perfectly. She entered the Juilliard School at just eight years old!

Illustration by Sabrena Khadija

ILHAN OMAR

A girl called Ilhan was told she had the spirit of a mighty queen. She broke boundaries as the first Somali American woman to be a US representative.

Illustration by Alessandra De Cristofaro

JAWAHIR JEWELS ROBLE

Once upon a time, there was a girl known as JJ who played soccer any chance she had. Later, JJ became the first female Muslim soccer referee.

Illustration by Veronica Ruffato

JOSEPHINE BAKER

There once was a girl who dazzled audiences and fought for equality. Josephine was an entertainer, French Resistance agent, and civil rights activist.

Illustration by Tyla Mason

LUPITA NYONG'O

Lupita was an adult when she admitted she wanted to be an actor. She won an Oscar and used her platform to address many important issues and celebrate Blackness.

Illustration by Monica Ahanonu

MERLENE JOYCE OTTEY

Once there was a girl named Merlene who ran like the wind. Her Olympic medal was the first to be won by a Caribbean woman.

Illustration by Luisa Rivera

NADINE BURKE HARRIS

There once was a girl who wanted to be a pediatrician. As California's first surgeon general, Nadine helped kids deal with toxic stress.

Illustration by Veronica Carratello

PNINA TAMANO-SHATA

Pnina was a Jewish girl born in Ethiopia. As a lawyer, she fought against discrimination.

Illustration by Olivia Fields

RAPELANG RABANA

There once was a girl who wanted to be an entrepreneur. Rapelang started a company to help people do better in school and work.

Illustration by Michelle D'Urbano

RIHANNA

Once upon a time, there was a girl who loved to perform. Rihanna catapulted to stardom as a singer and created her own fashion and beauty lines.

Illustration by Jestenia Southerland

ROSE FORTUNE

Rose patrolled the waterfront to make sure people obeyed the rules. She is now recognized as Canada's first female police officer.

Illustration by Sabrena Khadija

SURYA BONALY

When Surya skated, she made art on the ice. She created a daring signature move that made history in figure skating.

Illustration by Juliette Léveillé

TIMNIT GEBRU

Timnit grew up with a family who loved numbers and science. She soon created game-changing artificial intelligence programs.

Illustration by Aurélia Durand

VELMA SCANTLEBURY

Once there was a girl who wanted to be a doctor. Velma became the first female African American transplant surgeon.

Illustration by Irene Rinaldi

WRITE YOUR OWN STORY

Once upon a time, _____

_____

_____

_____

_____

_____

_____

_____

_____

_____

_____

_____

_____

_____

_____

_____

_____

_____

_____

_____

_____

_____

_____

DRAW YOUR OWN PORTRAIT

ACTIVITY TIME!

LET YOUR IMAGINATION SHINE!

Read about creators like singer Aretha Franklin and screenwriter Issa Rae. Then give your creativity a workout!

1. Aretha's song "Respect" became an anthem for women everywhere. Can you write a song that celebrates girls? Think of an empowering word or phrase, match it to a tune, and then SING!

2. Pretend you are a screenwriter like Issa. Imagine a scene between two people. What makes each character special and interesting? Write down the dialogue (the lines the characters say to each other). How do you make your scene exciting?

3. The portraits of Chido Govera and Patricia Bath were made with paper collages, and the portraits of Sanité Bélair and Suad Ali were created with watercolor paints. Pick a picture and create a portrait (of yourself or someone else) in the same style.

PLAN, BUILD, AND GROW!

Architect Beverly Loraine Greene, inventors Ruane and Sheila Jeter, and farmer Chido Govera are innovators. Innovators try out new ideas. They design buildings, invent gadgets, and carry out experiments.

1. Imagine the skyscraper, mall, or home of the future. Draw it! Add notes about the features that make your design clever and unique.

2. What toy, appliance, or other item do you think needs improvement? Step into the shoes of Ruane and Sheila, and invent a household object or gadget that is better than what exists today.

3. Ask a grown-up to help you buy and plant seeds—or you could try to raise mushrooms, just like Chido! Test out different amounts of water and light until you find the right combination to make your mushroom, flower, vegetable, or other plant thrive.

STRENGTHEN YOUR BODY AND YOUR MIND

Celebrate champions like tennis player Naomi Osaka, yoga instructor Jessamyn Stanley, and adventurer Barbara Hillary with these activities.

1. Athletes like Naomi need to stay limber and keep their muscles flexible so they don't get hurt when they run, jump, and move. Make a stretching plan that incorporates your arms, legs, and back. Stretch for 10 minutes every morning.

2. Physical endurance takes mental training too. Choose a mantra or affirmation that makes you feel strong and powerful. The next time you do yoga (like Jessamyn!), jump rope, or challenge a friend to a race, say the mantra to yourself and push yourself a little harder.

3. Grab a notebook and go on a nature walk with a grown-up. Write down what you see, smell, and hear on your journey. Like Barbara, jump up and down to celebrate making it to your destination!

LEAD THE WAY

Read about leaders like environmentalist Kristal Ambrose, journalists Ida B. Wells and Joy Reid, and the women of the Village of Umoja. Think about what their actions mean to you. Then tackle these challenges.

1. Follow Kristal's lead and choose an issue affecting Earth. How can you help? Come up with an action plan to present to friends, family, or a local group. Let your group know what they can do to make an impact. It's also okay if you'd rather lead from behind the scenes by joining an existing environmental group!

2. Think like Ida and Joy and write a news story about an issue that is important to you. Share it with your family, your teacher, your peers, or even your local paper.

3. Would you ever want to live in a special community like the Village of Umoja? If you were to set up your own community, what would it be like? Who would be invited to live in your community with you? What kinds of rules would you enact? Make a list!

GLOSSARY

AEROSPACE ENGINEERING (noun) — the field of engineering that deals with the development of aircraft and spacecraft

BIRACIAL (adjective) — having parents from two different racial groups

CIVIL RIGHTS MOVEMENT (noun) — a decades-long struggle for justice and equality for Black Americans that mainly took place in the 1950s and 1960s

COLONIAL (adjective) — this refers to the situation where one country exerts control over another country or area

COMPLEXION (noun) — the natural color of a person's skin

CONSERVATION (noun) — a movement focused on protecting animals, plants, and things found in nature and carefully using natural resources, such as water or trees, so they are not wasted

DISCRIMINATION (noun) — the unfair treatment of a person or group in a certain category, especially based on skin color, age, gender, or religion

DIVERSITY (noun) — including or involving people with differences in skin color, ethnicity, age, ability, appearance, culture, language, or religion

DYNASTY (noun) — a family or group who rules a country or region over a long period of time

DYSLEXIA (noun) — a learning issue where a person has trouble connecting letters, numbers, or symbols, making it more difficult to read, write, or spell

EMANCIPATION PROCLAMATION (noun) — an order issued by President Abraham Lincoln that freed "all persons held as slaves" within the US states that seceded from the Union in the lead-up to the Civil War

EQUITABLE (adjective) — fair and equal

EXECUTIVE PRODUCER (noun) — the person who finances or oversees the work of all other producers during the creation of a film, television show, or other performance

FOSTER (verb, adjective) — providing or receiving parental care without being related

HARLEM RENAISSANCE (noun) — a cultural explosion of Black literature, art, and music centered in the Harlem neighborhood of New York City during the 1920s and 1930s

HERITAGE (noun) — a person's sense of family identity handed down from previous generations and informed by ethnicity, cultural traditions, and other beliefs

HIJAB (noun) — a traditional head and neck covering worn by Muslim women

IMMIGRANT (noun) — a person who comes to a country to live there permanently

LATINX (adjective) — a gender-neutral alternative to "Latino" or "Latina" to describe someone of Latin American descent

LEGACY (noun) — a person's mark on the world that lives on after they stop working or pass away

LIBERATION (noun) — the act of setting someone free from something, such as oppression, enslavement, or imprisonment

MIDWIFE (noun) — someone trained to help pregnant women during childbirth

MIXED-RACE (adjective) — having parents from two or more racial groups

OPHTHALMOLOGY (noun) — a branch of medicine focused on the study and treatment of eye disorders and diseases

PARLIAMENT (noun) — an elected group of people who make laws in certain types of governments

PHYSICS (noun) — the branch of science that focuses on energy, matter, motion, and force

PSYCHOLOGY (noun) — the study of the human mind and behavior

RACISM (noun) — a belief that certain racial groups are superior or inferior to others, often leading to unfair or violent treatment of people based on their skin color or ethnicity

REFUGEE (noun) — a person who is forced to leave their country because of war, exile, or natural disaster or for political or religious reasons

REVOLUTION (noun) — when people attempt to overthrow a government

SECOND-GENERATION (adjective) — referring to the native-born children of immigrants

SEGREGATION (noun) — the act of isolating or separating people from one another based on skin color, religion, economic class, or another factor

SHARECROPPER (noun) — a farmer who raises crops for the landowner in exchange for a place to live and some (often small) portion of the money earned from the crops

SOCIAL JUSTICE (noun) — the view that everyone deserves equal access to wealth, privileges, and opportunities

STEREOTYPE (noun) — an unfair or untrue idea or depiction of another person or group of people

TRANSGENDER (adjective) — when a person's gender identity is not the same as the one assigned at birth

UNANIMOUS (adjective) — when all the members of a group are in total agreement on a decision

UNION (noun) — a group of workers who band together to protect their working rights

ABOUT THE AUTHORS

CASHAWN THOMPSON (foreword) is the brilliant mind behind Black Girls Are Magic and the hashtag #BlackGirlMagic. She believes in the phenomenal power and skill of Black women and girls. A passionate advocate of the work, will, and wonder of Black women, CaShawn champions their many causes online and in her everyday life. She lives right outside her hometown of Washington, DC, in Mount Rainier, Maryland, with her husband, two cats, and the various children and grandchildren who visit daily.

LILLY WORKNEH (editor, author) is an award-winning journalist who is passionate about impactful storytelling. She served as the editor-in-chief at Blavity News, where she directed the platform's mission to unpack and celebrate the many aspects of the Black millennial community. She previously led HuffPost Black Voices and is a *Forbes* 30 Under 30 honoree. Lilly is a Rebel Girl who wholeheartedly believes powerful stories can shift perspectives, expand imagination, and deepen understanding, helping to build a better future for all of us.

DIANA ODERO (author) is a writer living in Nairobi, Kenya, with bylines in many lifestyle, business, and travel publications. Curious to explore the world, she spent her time learning on different continents, earning her bachelor's and master's degrees from Chapman University (Orange, California) and University of Westminster (London, England), respectively. She is passionate about seeing her fellow women succeed and has spent the majority of her career writing about great women doing amazing things! An aspiring cat lady, Diana enjoys travel, reading, pastries, and a long stretch of beach.

JESTINE WARE (author) is a QPOC grant writer at the human rights organization Heartland Alliance by day and a stellar freelance editor, writer, and writing coach by night. She's edited kidlit titles *Madam C. J. Walker Builds a Business*, *Ada Lovelace Cracks the Code*, *Dr. Wangari Maathai Plants a Forest*, and *Junko Tabei Masters the Mountains*. Her comics, poems, stories, and activities have been featured in *Ladybug*, *Babybug*, *Spider*, *Cobblestone*, *Muse*, *Click*, and *Cicada* magazines and on *Good Night Stories for Rebel Girls: The Podcast*. In every project Jestine undertakes, she's passionate about supporting those who don't see themselves represented accurately—particularly communities of color, LGBTQIA+ folks, and people with disabilities. Originally from New York, Jestine lives in Chicago with her two feathered children, Owl and Sunny. In her spare time, she's a book afficionado, comic book enthusiast, gardener, avid puzzler, and dabbler in writing afrofuturist science fiction, fairy tales, and nonfiction short stories.

SONJA THOMAS (author) always wanted to be a writer, but she was afraid. So she became an accountant instead. One day, she said "enough!" and finally pursued her dreams. Now she writes stories for children of all ages, often featuring brave, everyday girls doing extraordinary things. Her debut middle grade novel, *Sir Fig Newton and the Science of Persistence*, is scheduled to publish in spring 2022 from Aladdin/Simon & Schuster. Originally from central Florida, she moved across the country and is now "keeping it weird" in the Pacific Northwest.

ILLUSTRATORS

Sixty-four extraordinary Black women and nonbinary artists who come from all over the world created the portraits of the trailblazing Rebel figures in this book. Here they are.

ACACIA RODRIGUEZ, USA, 113

Acacia is a nonbinary femme dudebro who illustrates for plants, nice animals, and people. Their main focus is in bringing a radically inclusive neon aesthetic to a visual project near you!

ADESEWA ADEKOYA, USA, 47

Adesewa is a Nigerian American illustrator who illustrates a vast array of diverse characters with elements of ethereality and fantasy.

ADRIANA BELLET, SWEDEN, 85, 91

Adriana is an editorial illustrator who delights in painting spirited faces and colorful spaces. She draws and paints for various international publications for both digital and print projects.

AISHA AKEJU, USA, 77, 169

Aisha currently works as a freelance illustrator and designer, creating book covers and promotional images for independent presses, publishing houses, and self-published authors.

ALEXANDRA BOWMAN, USA, 103, 217

Alexandra is an artist, illustrator, designer, muralist, and educator based in Oakland, California. Her clients include the *New York Times*, Penguin Random House, and Patagonia.

ALICIA ROBINSON, USA, 81, 151

Alicia is an illustrator and animator who enjoys creating fun, authentic stories with characters who inspire all audiences. Her work is often influenced by her identity, nostalgia, and pop culture.

ALLEANNA HARRIS, USA, 87, 101

Alleanna is an illustrator living in New Jersey who has been drawing for as long as she can remember. As a kid, she would draw on every page of her mom's legal pads and doodle on her notebooks at school and the programs at church. She graduated with honors from the University of the Arts with a BFA in animation.

AMARI MITNAUL, USA, 51, 220

Amari is an illustrator and character designer who is extremely grateful to be a part of this collective of artists. This is Amari's first published project.

ANJINI MAXWELL, SWEDEN, 181, 193

Anjini is a freelance illustrator who enjoys working with various colors. She's previously worked with companies such as *Billboard* magazine, *Glamour*, AARP, and Verizon.

ASHLEIGH CORRIN, USA, 57, 201

Ashleigh is an award-winning children's book illustrator. Her appreciation for philanthropic work and acts of service shaped her dream of creating art to uplift, teach, inspire, and invigorate the minds of youth and the young at heart.

AURÉLIA DURAND, DENMARK, 39, 59, 223

Aurélia's art is a vivid celebration of diversity. She dedicates her artistic voice to matters involving representation. Her work has been featured in advertising campaigns, galleries, and editorial magazines, and her clients include Nike, the *New Yorker*, Facebook, and more.

BRIA NICOLE, USA, 205

Bria is a visual artist and illustrator of lifestyle imagery and portraits. She is known for her print collections and has also illustrated for brands and retail shops.

CAMILLA RU, UK, 211

Camilla is a Zimbabwean-born illustrator who loves creating colorful illustrations for books, magazines, albums, and more. Her work incorporates her love of vibrant colors and passion for connecting people.

CHERISE HARRIS, BARBADOS, 45

Cherise spent much of her childhood writing stories and making art. She currently lives in Barbados with her husband and daughter.

CLAIRE IDERA, NIGERIA, 93

Claire is an exceptional designer and artist with a background in architecture and fashion. She has illustrated for Hugo Boss, Lagos Fashion Week, and other publications and fashion brands.

COZBI A. CABRERA, USA, 67

Cozbi is a multimedia artist who creates handmade dolls and quilts, designs clothing, and writes and illustrates children's books. *Me & Mama* was awarded a Caldecott Honor and a Coretta Scott King Honor. *Exquisite: The Poetry and Life of Gwendolyn Brooks* was awarded a Coretta Scott King Honor and a Sibert Informational Award Honor.

DANIELLE ELYSSE MANN, USA, 149, 187

Danielle has created cover art, illustrations for children's books, and character designs for a children's clothing line, among other design work. She supports representation for the historically marginalized, especially women of color, and explores this as a narrative in her art practice.

DATA ORUWARI, NIGERIA, 61, 143

Data is a Nigerian-raised, Brooklyn-based illustrator, visual artist, and UX designer passionate about how creativity can help shape society. Her illustration style is a dynamic blend of her love for both traditional and digital media, with subjects depicting African culture and African women. She has illustrated for brands like Google and has been recognized by *Business Insider* as one of the 36 rising stars of Madison Avenue who are revolutionizing advertising.

ELIZABETH MONTERO SANTA, DOMINICAN REPUBLIC, 109

Elizabeth is a Dominican illustrator residing in Barcelona who seeks to give visibility to Black women and social injustices through her illustrations.

FANESHA FABRE, USA, 171, 189, 221

Fanesha is a Brooklyn-based, Dominican-born multimedia artist and the daughter of Dominican painter and sculptor Vicente Fabre. In her illustrations, she celebrates her experiences as a Latina living in New York City. Her illustrations capture and elevate her everyday surroundings with vibrant colors. She's worked with companies like Mitú, Twitter, Starbucks, and Whole Foods and was featured in Fierce by Mitú, Buzzfeed, *Latina* magazine online, *Complex*, and Telemundo.

GABRIELLE FLUDD, USA, 107

Gabrielle graduated from the Savannah College of Art and Design with a major in illustration. She lives in Connecticut and teaches art when she isn't illustrating for her freelance clients.

GABRIELLE TESFAYE, USA, 199

Gabrielle is an interdisciplinary artist versed in painting, film, and animation. Her work is rooted in cultural storytelling, folklore, and collective histories from her Ethiopian and Jamaican heritage.

JEANETTA GONZALES, USA, 63, 175, 217

Jeanetta captures moods and moments through bold statements of inspiration, positivity, and beauty. She has created artwork for the *New York Times*, Facebook, and the California State Lottery.

JOELLE AVELINO, CONGO, 153

Joelle is a London-based Congolese and Angolan illustrator. She has illustrated numerous publications and worked with many leading brands.

JOHNALYNN HOLLAND, USA, 37, 207

Johnalynn is an illustrator and writer living in Washington, DC.

JONELL JOSHUA, USA, 173, 179

Jonell is an illustrator based in Brooklyn, New York, and her illustrations have been recognized by the Society of Illustrators and American Illustration: International Motion Art Awards.

KATELUN C. BREWSTER, TRINIDAD AND TOBAGO, 29

Katelun has done commissioned graphic art, fantasy-style illustrations, and portraits for both regional and international clients. She loves bright, saturated colors against melanin-rich complexions.

KEISHA MORRIS, USA, 167, 197

Keisha is an illustrator living and working in Maryland. When she is not drawing, she loves spending time with her wife, daughter, and two crazy cats!

KEISHA OKAFOR, USA, 131, 139

Keisha is an artist and designer who creates vibrant illustrations and patterns for various brands, including IGN, Piccolina Kids, and AARP.

KELSEE THOMAS, USA, 25, 43

Kelsee is a freelance illustrator working in Los Angeles and originally from Dayton, Ohio. She spends her time listening to too much music, binging Netflix nightly, and trying to finish the books she keeps buying for her ever-growing library.

KETURAH ARIEL, USA, 23, 121

Keturah is an artist and number one *New York Times* best-selling illustrator known for creating vibrant images that are relatable and distinguishable. She is passionate about creating art that inspires, uplifts, and advocates for her community. Keturah has been praised for her colorful, illustrative style that brings the story to life and resonates with the viewer.

KIM HOLT, USA, 55, 129

Kim's main goal as an artist is to create images that bring back memories and make people recall events in their own life or think of someone they know. Her style is full of color and emotion, and she has an interest in projects that make people think and talk. She has signed on to illustrate her first picture book.

KYLIE AKIA ERWIN, USA, 145, 163

Kylie is a digital freelance illustrator and painter residing in Chicago, Illinois. Her work creates a narrative of juxtaposition by the use of color, subject, and content.

LAUWAART, MARTINIQUE, 209

From her quest for identity to the celebration of her origins, through that perpetual stylistic and technical artistic exploration, Lauwaart creates art that is an invitation to self-expression that is addressed first to Black women of this time, then to the world.

LINDSEY BAILEY, USA, 73, 191

Lindsey is an artist and illustrator who has worked on editorial illustrations, books, portraits, and fine art. Her work focuses on the representation of Black people, specifically women, and NBIPOC.

LYDIA MBA, SPAIN, 31

Lydia is an Afro-Spanish illustrator with a mission as an artist to create more diverse narratives in children's books and representation in art. She has created work for the publishing, editorial, and game industries.

MARINA VENANCIO, BRAZIL, 17

Marina always loved drawing and dreamed of being an illustrator to make drawings for books like this one. She is a regular girl who has had to be rebellious sometimes to achieve her dream.

MAYA EALEY, USA, 35, 117

Maya is a designer and illustrator based in sunny Oakland, California, whose love for color, technology, representation, and nostalgia is reflected throughout her work.

MIA SAINE, USA, 137, 215

Mia is a nonbinary Black illustrator and designer from Memphis, Tennessee. They enjoy normalizing and amplifying the empowerment and happiness of minorities and their experiences.

MONET KIFNER, USA, 71, 157

Monet is a freelance illustrator based in Buffalo, New York. Her work combines digital and traditional media to create psychedelic, colorful motifs that adorn her figures.

MYRIAM CHERY, CANADA, 79

Myriam is an illustrator from Québec in Canada. She loves to illustrate colorful landscapes and adorable characters that highlight the happiness of childhood.

NAKI NARH, UK, 21, 141

Naki is an artist of Ghanaian descent from two homes: Accra and London. Her work currently plays with explosions of color and patterns as distinctive features that mark a rapidly evolving signature style. These ideas are expressed through the mediums of ink and acrylic on paper, digital painting, and canvas.

NAOMI ANDERSON-SUBRYAN, UK, 65, 159

Naomi is a London-based illustrator and maker who works largely in collage. Naomi's collaged illustrations are pieced together using brightly colored, hand-painted paper.

NAOMI SILVERIO, USA, 97

Naomi is an illustrator with a passion for portraits and hand lettering.

NICOLE MILES, THE BAHAMAS, 115, 125, 135, 221

Nicole is an illustrator from the Bahamas living in the United Kingdom with her pet snake and human boyfriend. Her clients include Adobe, Buzzfeed, Google, Penguin Random House, and more.

NOA DENMON, USA, 203

Noa is an award-winning illustrator who loves to uplift and depict the stories of the underrepresented and hopes to create work that displays humanity in all its differences.

NOKWANDA THEMBA, SOUTH AFRICA, 195

Nokwanda is a woman of color, visual artist, and illustrator from South Africa, as well as a member of AWID. She has worked with artists in the United States, Canada, Japan, and across Africa. Her work has been featured in numerous publications, exhibitions, and galleries.

NYANZA D, UK, 165
Nyanza is a London-based artist who uses vintage pop art and comic book conventions to depict Black women as modern muses in her work. She has illustrated for a range of global brands, such as MTV, Amazon, Tumblr, and more.

OCTAVIA JACKSON, USA, 119, 133
Octavia has created illustrations for various books and publications. She became passionate about illustration when she saw the underrepresentation of women of color like herself in the world of art. Also a local activist, Octavia uses her artwork as a fundraiser for marginalized groups in her community.

OLIVIA FIELDS, USA, 41, 185, 223
Olivia is an illustrator and cartoonist based in New York City. Select clients include Google, HP, the *New York Times*, NPR, PBS, *Variety*, and Xbox.

ONYINYE IWU, UK, 161
Onyinye was born to Nigerian parents in Italy, where she spent her childhood. She moved to the UK as a teenager. She is an illustrator and educator who loves drawing and writing for children and enjoys sharing her African heritage in her work.

QUEENBE MONYEI, USA, 83
Queenbe is a digital artist and gif creator. She is passionate about drawing marginalized groups in everyday situations through the use of bold colors, hoping to shed light on their humanity.

RENIKE, NIGERIA, 111
Morenike Olusanya, popularly known as Renike, is a Nigerian visual artist with a background in graphic design. She works as a freelance graphic artist, traditional artist, and illustrator. She enjoys creating art that centers and portrays the lives of Black girls and women. She has worked with brands such as Dark & Lovely, Routledge, and Penguin Random House, among others.

SANIYYAH ZAHID, USA, 89, 99
Saniyyah is an illustrator aiming to showcase Black and brown women in her artwork. She is primarily known as Peachpod on Instagram and Twitter, and her biggest aspiration is to start her own web-comic series.

SARAH LOULENDO, FRANCE, 49, 127
Sarah has made illustrations for several children's books and also for magazines, frescoes, and textile patterns.

SARAH MADDEN, UK, 27, 123
Sarah is a UK-based graphic designer and illustrator with a passion for bold and colorful artwork. Her work aims to inspire and empower individuals, focusing on themes of personal well-being and mental health.

SHAREE MILLER, USA, 147, 177
Sharee is an author, illustrator, and designer located on the East Coast of the United States. Her art is fresh and full of joy. It encourages all who view it to smile. She works in traditional and digital media.

SIMONE MARTIN-NEWBERRY, USA, 105
Simone is an illustrator and graphic designer whose work is guided by a love of color, texture, movement, and rhythm. She has created art for the *New York Times*, the *Guardian* (US), *Emergence Magazine*, Chronicle Books, and many others. Originally from Los Angeles, she currently lives, works, and gardens in Chicago.

TAYLOR MCMANUS, USA, 19, 95
Taylor is an illustrator and educator based in northern Virginia with a bachelor of fine arts degree in illustration and a masters of art in teaching from the Maryland Institute College of Art.

TEQUITIA ANDREWS, USA, 75
Tequitia is an artist and illustrator from Richmond, Virginia. Her work features and celebrates women of color.

TIFFANY BAKER, USA, 183, 213
Tiffany is a Brooklyn-based visual artist working in oil, acrylic, and digital media. Marked by vibrant palettes and considered attention to her subjects' grooming, Tiffany merges the somber, the regal, and the mundane, bringing forth each subject's intensity. In her portraiture, Tiffany turns life experiences into emotive visual expressions that reimagine trauma, embed messages of connection, and celebrate her identity as a Black woman.

TONI D. CHAMBERS, USA, 33, 53
Toni is an illustrator and graphic novelist from New Haven, Connecticut.

TRUDI-ANN HEMANS, JAMAICA, 69
Trudi is a Jamaican-born, Atlanta-based artist who loves illustrating whimsical pieces with surreal botanical elements, dreamy color palettes, and diverse characters.

VALENCIA SPATES, USA, 155
Valencia is an illustrator and storyboard artist who works in TV animation in Los Angeles.

 # LEARN MORE!

BOOKS

Books Featuring Women in This Book

- *Bessie Coleman: Daring Stunt Pilot* by Trina Robbins
- *Bessie Stringfield: Tales of the Talented Tenth, no. 2* by Joel Christian Gill
- *Clara Hale: Mother to Those Who Needed One* by Bob Italia
- *Changing the Equation: 50+ US Black Women in STEM* by Tonya Bolden
- *The Doctor with an Eye for Eyes: The Story of Dr. Patricia Bath* by Julia Finley Mosca
- *Fly High! The Story of Bessie Coleman* by Louise Borden and Mary Kay Kroeger
- *Gabby Douglas (Amazing Athletes)* by Jon M. Fishman
- *In Her Hands: The Story of Sculptor Augusta Savage* by Alan Schroeder
- *Leaders Like Us: Sister Rosetta Tharpe (Rourke Educational Media)* by J. P. Miller
- *Let It Shine: Stories of Black Women Freedom Fighters* by Andrea Davis Pinkney
- *She Persisted: Florence Griffith Joyner* by Chelsea Clinton and Rita Williams-Garcia
- *Shirley Chisholm (You Should Meet)* by Laurie Calkhoven
- *Simone Manuel: Swimming Star* by Heather E. Schwartz
- *The Story of Kamala Harris: A Biography Book for New Readers* by Tonya Leslie, PhD
- *Sylvia and Marsha Start a Revolution: The Story of the Trans Women of Color Who Made LGBTQ+ History* by Joy Michael Ellison
- *Viola Desmond: A Hero for Us All* by Sarah Howden
- *Young, Gifted and Black: Meet 52 Black Heroes from Past and Present* by Jamia Wilson
- *Yours for Justice, Ida B. Wells: The Daring Life of a Crusading Journalist* by Philip Dray
- *Women in Gaming: 100 Professionals of Play* by Meagan Marie
- *Who Was Aretha Franklin?* by Nico Medina
- *Who Was Ida B. Wells?* by Sarah Fabiny

Books by Women Featured in This Book

- *The Big Box* by Toni Morrison with Slade Morrison
- *Change Sings: A Children's Anthem* by Amanda Gorman
- *Corduroy Takes a Bow* by Viola Davis
- *Explorers: Amazing Tales of the World's Greatest Adventurers* by Nellie Huang, with a foreword by Barbara Hillary
- *A Long Way from the Strawberry Patch: The Life of Leah Chase* by Carol Allen with Leah Chase
- *The Proudest Blue: A Story of Hijab and Family* by Ibtihaj Muhammad with S. K. Ali
- *Raising the Bar* by Gabrielle Douglas
- *Remember: The Journey to School Integration* by Toni Morrison
- *Superheroes Are Everywhere* by Kamala Harris

WEBSITES

1000 Black Girl Books Resource Guide
grassrootscommunityfoundation.org/1000-black-girl-books-resource-guide

Algorithmic Justice League
ajl.org

Bahamas Plastic Movement
bahamasplasticmovement.org

Black Girls Code
blackgirlscode.com

Black Lives Matter
blacklivesmatter.com

Conservation Through Public Health
ctph.org

The Future of Hope Foundation
thefutureofhope.org

Miss Rizos
missrizos.com

Rollin Funky
rollinfunkyblog.com

Stemettes
stemettes.org (UK only)

Therapy for Black Girls
therapyforblackgirls.com

Umoja Village
umojawomen.or.ke

TURN UP THE MUSIC!

With the help of a grown-up, look up songs by or videos of Aretha Franklin, Insooni, MC Soffia, Nandi Bushell, Poly Styrene, Queendom, Rosetta Tharpe, Roxanne Shanté, Susana Baca, and Tania J. León Ferrán.

LISTEN TO REBELS!

Go online and find TED Talks by and interviews with Adriana Barbosa, Amanda Gorman, Andrea Jenkins, Anne-Marie Imafidon, Joy Buolamwini, Judith Jamison, Kimberly Bryant, Leah Chase, Sonia Guimarães, and the trio of Alicia Garza, Opal Tometi, and Patrisse Cullors.

PODCASTS

Activist, You!

African Folktales: Traditional Bedtime Stories for the Modern Kid

Good Night Stories for Rebel Girls

Hey Black Child: The Podcast

MORE FROM REBEL GIRLS

Let the stories of more real-life women entertain and inspire you!
Each volume in the Good Night Stories series includes 100 tales
of extraordinary women.

Check out these mini books too! Each one contains 25 tales of
talented women, along with a quiz and some engaging activities.